HARD CORE ROAD- SHOW

HARD CORE ROAD-SHOW

A SCREENWRITER'S DIARY

NOEL S. BAKER
FOREWORD BY BRUCE McDONALD

Carlo:
Let's go down to Hollywood (and shoot some people)
There'll always be Ottawa.
Noel.

Anansi

a spider line book

Copyright © 1997 by Noel S. Baker

All rights reserved. No part of this publication may be reproduced or transmitted in any form or by any means, electronic or mechanical, including photocopying, recording, or any information storage and retrieval system, without permission in writing from the publisher.

Published in 1997 by
House of Anansi Press Limited
1800 Steeles Avenue West, Concord, ON
Canada L4K 2P3

Distributed in Canada by
General Distribution Services Inc.
30 Lesmill Road
Toronto, Canada M3B 2T6
Tel. (416) 445-3333
Fax (416) 445-5967
e-mail: Customer.Service@ccmailgw.genpub.com

Canadian Cataloguing in Publication Data

Baker, Noel S.
Hard core roadshow

"A Spider line book"
ISBN 0-88784-584-3

1. Hard core logo (Motion picture). 2. Baker, Noel S.
3. McDonald, Bruce, 1959– . 4. Screenwriters – Canada –
Biography. I. Title.

PN1997.H373B34 1997   791.43'72   C97-930115-7

Cover design: Bill Douglas @ The Bang
Printed and bound in Canada
Typesetting: ECW Type & Art, Oakville

House of Anansi Press gratefully acknowledges the support of the Canada Council and the Ontario Arts Council in the development of writing and publishing in Canada.

For Siobhan and Emma,
who make my heart go boom

FOREWORD

I've always wanted to be a writer, but I'm still too timid to go the distance. I've tried poems, short stories, screenplays, and the results, especially the screenplays, have been bad. Quite bad, so I've been told. So, I became a movie director as opposed to a writer/director, the tag most Canadian filmmakers go by.

My own writing was probably bad because I was always in a hurry, never taking the time to really smell the moment; plot completely overshadowed character, and I always thought the answer was more important than the question. Add to that a shaky sense of structure and movie clichés heaped upon tiny rumors of the truth and you can clearly see my need to find a real writer to work with.

Noel Baker is a real screenwriter. So are Don McKellar and Semi Chellas, two other wonderfully original collaborators of mine. In this book, Noel explains the beginnings of *Hard Core Logo* far better than I ever could, so let me just tell you why I believe he is a really great screenwriter. He reads. Always has, always will. He researches like crazy, digging up all kinds of wild and woolly details that add tremendous verve to the story. He has opinions. He is curious about the world he lives in and the worlds that he would like to live in. He can tell you the difference between irony and mockery — both very useful tools for living in any world. He is not precious. He's very passionate about what he does. He tells stories free of wank. He has a big ego and is very insecure and admits it. He believes that screenwriting is not only the art of visualizing strong ideas and characters but it is very much a craft that must be studied and learned and practiced and practiced and practiced. And he's not afraid to go the distance — whatever it takes.

When I first read Michael Turner's book *Hard Core Logo*, I thought it would be a cakewalk to adapt for film, perhaps because it spoke to me so honestly and clearly. Little did I realize all the demands that the art and craft of screenwriting put on time and space. With his screenplay, Noel had to figure out how to carve out a strong narrative from a book of set lists, song lyrics, phone conversations, diary entries, and sublime poetry; he had to figure out how to set up the characters and the story in the first reel, how to write with low-budget in mind, how to make scenes, subtext, conflict, irony, etc., visible and memorable within a linear ninety-minute timeframe — in short, how to write cinema. The script is the treasure map, it's the instruction booklet for three-dimensional chess. The great Russian director Tarkovsky says making movies is like sculpting in time.

The production proved to be quite a battle, and so did the writing, a battle that Noel fought in solitude in the arena of his tiny workroom. I'd bring him coffee from the Second Cup around the corner on College Street, or be his sounding board during various drinking sessions, or provide moral support over the phone. In the end, he was alone to do the dirty deed. My only real job was to keep him convinced that we were gonna roll film through the camera in the foreseeable future. That was a huge motivator for Noel, because for the first time he had a shot at having a produced screenplay.

I like having the writer on set, and it's a tradition I haven't broken yet, but it's kinda like inviting the priest to come along on your honeymoon. Noel was the priest during the *Hard Core* honeymoon and the days and nights went great because Noel was always there to remind me of our initial intentions. He kept his clothes on most of the time while preaching that God is in the details.

I am lucky and privileged to have worked with Noel and become his friend. I am luckier still to be scheming a new project with him. I hope you enjoy Noel's story of the making of our cool little movie. I did. And I was there. Here you are. Go.

Bruce McDonald
Twitch City, January 1997

HELLO, MY NAME IS . . .

Year in and year out vast forests are razed and pulped so that the dreams of unproduced yet ever hopeful screenwriters can be printed, copied, circulated, read, perchance bought, and — the dream come true! — transmuted to a strip of material made of the boiled hooves and horns of beasts slaughtered by the million.

The following diary tells the story of one screenwriter's environmentally degrading dream coming true with the production of a fiercely independent rock 'n' roll road movie called *Hard Core Logo*. What is true of the movie is also by and large true of the story of its making: it is a harrowing tale of party-going, bar-hopping, band-watching, hard rocking, vandalizing, chain-smoking, stripper-ogling, road trips, accidents, arrests, and other forms of cultural research.

For those in search of more useful information about *Hard Core Logo*, screenwriting, and filmmaking in general, this diary is also a detailed chronicle of long months of scripting, of creative decisions made and abandoned, of gruelling pitch meetings and casting sessions, of the struggle to secure financing in an era of cutbacks and economic caution, of the pressures of production and post-production, of the release of the film and its reception by audiences and critics. In all, it covers more than two years of my life, from my first meeting with director Bruce McDonald in the summer of

1994, to the fall of 1996 with the award-winning *Hard Core Logo* about to leave its Canadian home and venture forth into the wide world to seek its fortune.

The perspective of this book is fiercely screenwriterly and personal, and I take full responsibility for any irresponsible rants or reflections. Many others worked long and hard on *HCL* and had as much impact on its final shape as I did. I try to represent their actions, characters, and involvement as accurately as possible here, but I don't expect anyone to see things exactly as I did and I am sure that some of my colleagues would give you wildly different versions of certain events were you to buy them drinks and ask them if my account is true. If I prove in the pages to follow to be a poor servant of the truth, I can only shrug and ask, "whose truth?"

Noel Baker
Toronto, January 1997

1.

WHO THE HELL DO YOU THINK YOU ARE?

21 July 1994, Toronto

I am so fucking broke. Look up broke in the thesaurus and you could well find, right there with bankrupt bust destitute impecunious impoverished penurious skint strapped tapped and other synonyms, my name.

I am so fucking broke. I am so fucking Noel.

The root of the problem is simple: I am a writer who specializes in the screenplay. Along with most of the world's "screenwriters," none of my scripts has ever been produced. So I tend not to make any money from them. I get the odd grant and script development loan. I take the odd odd-job. Odd little amounts of money trickle in from time to time, just enough to keep my girlfriend Siobhan from giving me up for, well, broke.

Days like today, the bank balance down to single digits, I have these horrible panic attacks and find myself cold-calling producers of shitty little Canadian TV series to announce my availability as a writer. The rationale: starting way down here will yield the fastest results. I tell them that I love their wily plots, complex characters, the Important Issues their shows Explore week after week. I'll say anything, take anything. Anything. Today I'd write for *The Littlest Hobo* if it was still in production. If they'd let me. They never do, though. I pull out all the stops trying to sell out, but no one ever gives me the chance. So my integrity remains intact at day's end whether I like it or not.

Today could be the day, though. Just heard about a new Canadian series in development that sounds just shitty enough to merit a cold call from an unproduced screenwriter desperate for work. I make the call. And my God, the shock: I am rewarded with an invitation to drop by for a little chat with a producer who sounds downright warm and receptive. Cut to . . .

22 July 1994

Interior. A producer's office with exposed brick walls. Day.

Steamy, sweltering summer heat, shirt's stuck to my back (lacking bus fare, I've walked here). I sit across from the warm and receptive Brian Dennis in the offices of Shadow Shows, on the fourth floor of a converted warehouse owned by the director Norman Jewison.

The director Bruce McDonald.

— who the hell do you think you are ? —

Brian is a producer working with Bruce McDonald. Bruce is Norman's protégé and the director of *Roadkill*, *Highway 61*, and *Dance Me Outside*. With one or two exceptions, Bruce is the only English-Canadian filmmaker I can think of who makes "fun" movies. I'm here to shoot the breeze with Brian re: writing opportunities on *The Rez*, the TV series they're developing out of the just finished *Dance Me Outside*. Got all these episode ideas I want to pitch. Brian, however, is preoccupied trying to figure out why my name rings a bell.

Suddenly the lightbulb goes on, he grabs this fresh small-press paperback off a shelf, slides it across the desk. Book's called *Hard Core Logo*, by some guy I've never heard of, Michael Turner.

Totally spooky I've chosen this moment to drop by, Brian says.

Spooky?

I look at the book. Sticky note bearing my name curls from the jacket. Brian explains that Bruce has just optioned this *Hard Core Logo* book and that my name sort of came up in discussions about possible screenwriters. I assure him that aside from a very small circle of friends and relatives, not a soul knows I even exist. I network for shit and write in the wilderness, when not busy plotting my escape to the States. So what's my name doing stuck to that little book? Brian asks if the name Keith Porteous means anything.

Well now. Keith's one of the few, the proud, the brave. A roommate from ten years ago in Vancouver, an old pal. Manages bands: 54–40 and Mae Moore among others. He's also sort of a virtuoso networker, facilitator, connector of talents, a fixer, a knower of shitloads of people. There's probably only one guy in the whole world who could hook me up with Bruce McDonald in this way, and that guy is Keith.

Yeah but the thing is, says Brian, still pondering the spookiness of my timing, I wasn't sure where to find you so if you hadn't walked in right about now, I'd probably never have bothered tracking you down.

In other words this is my lucky day.

Brian tells me the book's about a Vancouver punk band but that's as far as he gets when Bruce shambles in. There it is, the wispy long hair, the scruffy beard, the black shirt, ripped jeans, army boots. The guy who posed atop a Harley in leather and bandanna for *Playback*. The bad boy of Canadian film. The guy who promised an audience of Canadian film biz worthies he'd spend his $25,000 Toronto Film Festival/Citytv award for *Roadkill* on a "big chunk of hash." That was back in 1989 or so. The reputation has done nothing but grow since then. Guy gets a lot of Canadian press. He's as close to famous as Canadian directors get without leaving for Hollywood.

Brian makes the introduction. Friendly handshake. In the flesh Bruce is smart, funny, soft spoken, gentle, and very positive about everything. His eyes narrow to slits when he smiles, and he smiles a lot. Looks like he spends lots of time enjoying himself. I'm thinking maybe he's still working his way through that chunk of hash, what with this affable stoner vibe. The guy is just so incredibly relaxed.

When Brian explains that I'm the guy on the sticky note on the book in my hand Bruce grins and says, "right on." We speak. He says "right on" several more times, then asks me to read the book and let him know if there's a decent movie in it. I give him a sample script I wrote with my pal David Griffith called *Gotterdammerung*. An apocalyptic rock 'n' roll zombie comedy. I explain the story quickly. He laughs, says "right on," promises to read it tonight, leaves.

I hit the boiling street, clutching my copy of *Hard Core Logo*. Thinking about this little twist of fate. Never did get around to pitching those episode ideas.

23 July 1994

I call Keith Porteous in Vancouver, thank him for making the contact and explain the circumstances. He gets pretty cosmic over the fact that I walked into Bruce's office unbidden, as if I was drawn there by some mysterious force. It's called poverty, I tell him.

Expensive long-distance chit-chat about serendipity, coincidence, destiny, fate, the ideas of the trippy physicist David Bohm as they apply to the *Hard Core Logo* "deal." Keith views business as a mystical subatomic process, full of subtle vibrations and Schrödingerian contingencies. I view things in terms of raw hope and dumb luck (which may well amount to the same thing).

Whether meant to be or not, the facts leading to this moment are these: Keith happened to be ligging at some downtown rooftop barbecue in Toronto last summer, happened to meet Bruce there, happened to strike up a fateful conversation about rock 'n' roll and movies, happened to tell Bruce about his buddy Michael Turner's book; Bruce happened to read it, love it, see its cinematic potential. He happened, eventually, to option it. Only two days ago, Keith happened to be talking to Brian Dennis and happened to mention my name as a possible screenwriter, and yesterday I just happened to walk into the office on unrelated business.

Now I happen to be sitting here looking at this book wondering if I can keep this daisychain of happy happenings happening. Keith is confident we'll be sitting side by side with a big bag of popcorn at the movie's premiere in one year. Year and a half, I say. He calls me a pessimist.

27 July 1994

Read *Hard Core Logo* twice more last night, bringing the number of read-throughs to five. Question remains: what the hell is it? Not a novel. Not exactly a poetry collection and not precisely a prose poem. It's more of a collage of fragments that conspire to form an absorbing narrative about this defunct Vancouver punk band (Hard Core Logo) who try to recapture lost glory by re-forming in the early 90s to go on an unplugged tour of Western Canada. The fragments are composed of song lyrics, letters, answering machine messages, diary entries, press release copy, confessions, interview excerpts, receipts and invoices, the odd picture. It's lean and spare, full of gaps and silences, the eloquence of things left unsaid. Think of mirror shards on rough pavement, reflecting bits of glorious sky. Bittersweet air of beauty in squalor, love among the ruins, etc.

The book has an intensely local sensibility, very specific to the politics of Vancouver. In a gorgeous, wet, generally well-heeled city on the edge of nowhere you'd think there'd be nothing to complain about punk-style, except maybe the rain. But Vancouver punk was amazingly robust, singular, cool, political. There was a tasty Enemy to take aim at, a provincial government run by Socred buffoons, in power throughout the punk years. Turner's book posits a band that took aim early and never quit blasting at the bastards. He's done a great job capturing the geist of the zeit.

There are some convenient aspects to having me adapt this book for the screen. I did much of my growing up in

──────── who the hell do you think you are ? ────────

The poet Michael Turner.

Vancouver, was there when punk hit, hung out on the edges of the local music scene in the early 80s, was deeply involved with CITR, the alternative radio station at UBC. When I should have been studying, I was going to punk gigs, interviewing bands, poking around in record stores, listening to obscure punk import singles, Joy Division bootlegs, demo tapes by local bands. I was hanging out with local musicians, getting stoned at the radio station, going to boozecans. I was busy showing up, busy being there. So I know a fair bit about this scene.

The book's characters remind me of people I've known. They're vivid composites of real musicians, probably Michael Turner's bandmates from Hard Rock Miners, the group he played in during the 80s, and DOA, the longest-lived and best known of the Vancouver punk bands. The members of

Hard Core Logo are demagogic lead singer Joe Dick (love the name), the temperamental guitarist Billy Tallent, the rational and bookish bass player John Oxenberger, and the archetypal loogan drummer, Pipefitter. The band was formed in Vancouver in 1977 when the characters were still in their teens. They are now in their early thirties, and none is entirely trained for post-rock 'n' roll life.

The fragmented story opens when Joe Dick is asked to reunite Hard Core Logo to perform a benefit concert for an eco-hippie environmental group, the Green World Coalition. Without the band to provide Joe a platform and an identity, he's just another moaning welfare case. So he thinks a reunion is a splendid idea. Joe manages to convince Billy and the others to do the benefit show, playing only acoustic instruments. The gig is a success, and this gets Joe thinking about a full reunion tour. Again he approaches the others, who overcome their reservations and decide to do it. A five-city tour of Western Canada is booked, and Hard Core Logo hit the road with high hopes.

On the road, with the guys cooped up in their lousy van, tensions mount. Bit by bit, through unusual little fragments, details, reminiscences, and regrets past problems bubble to the surface. The road takes its toll in the narrative present. The band's performances are up and down. A gig is canceled. With time to kill, they drop in on Joe's mentor, the retired punk legend Bucky Haight, who lives on a farm in Saskatchewan. Bucky tells them stories of his harrowing life in the rock 'n' roll fast lanes in New York and L.A. Bucky is an emblem of squandered potential and lost hope, of that which awaits the Hard Cores at the end of the rock 'n' roll road.

The band moves on and plays Saskatoon and Edmonton. There are further disasters and humiliations. The tour is doomed. The band is doomed, though Joe refuses to acknowledge this fact or give in to it. In Edmonton, last city on the tour, the journey at its nadir, Joe reams the guys out one by one: John for his suspicious diary writing (it's driving Pipe crazy with paranoia), Pipe for constantly whining and for taking a dump on his hotel bed in Regina, and Billy for calling Ed Festus, the band's sleazy former manager, whom Joe has banished from his life. Then a betrayal: Billy hears from Festus that he's been hired by a Seattle band. He announces on air during a college radio interview that he'll be leaving HCL forever after this show. The band breaks up once more, for the last time, after the show. Billy splits for Seattle and his new life. The others return to Vancouver, sadder but wiser for the final tour experience. Joe advertises for new musicians to form a "kick-ass rock 'n' roll band." The beat sort of goes on. End of story.

Book's front cover boasts a blurb from Art Bergmann: "The loudest book I've ever read about the hell-fire that is today's music business." Only problem for me is that it's just a whisper of a movie idea, maybe too lean and spare. It's wry, poignant, and clever literature, loaded with bittersweet epiphanies. Obviously I'm at home with this material, but can I make a feature script of it?

8 August 1994

Siobhan is most pleased to see me gainfully employed, for once, at this trade. Spent a week procrastinating, then a week writing the treatment. Twenty-two pages that hit the pavement running. I am pleased. Found a few linking devices, and otherwise just transcribed the book as is into a workable cinematic form. It's a four-pronged documentary-style narrative about the four members of Hard Core Logo who, when not acting their way through some verité style scenes, spend a lot of time facing the camera, confessing, blabbing, gossiping, stabbing each other in the back. Dead simple, really. Must thank Turner for writing so little yet suggesting so much. Adapting novels to the screen is usually a process of subtraction. In this case it's not and I've had a great time filling in the blanks.

I drop the treatment off at the office and blurt out my take on the material to Brian. In the middle of this pitch, Bruce walks in, cuts me off. Just wants to let me know he stayed up last night reading *Gotterdammerung*, and he loved it. So much so that he read it twice. Wow. Flattering. But more than this, a director after my own heart, right down to a taste for grandiose end-of-the-world zombie pictures. Could be the start of a halfway decent relationship.

14 August 1994

Bruce calls, doesn't mince words. He's read the treatment and he loves it! Maybe Keith's right and there is a subatomic Santa Claus at work here. This is too easy. When's the catch going to come? It always does. I've written eight feature scripts on spec, some of which have almost been made, but there's always a snag. Things don't just fall together like this.

Bruce talks about process, suggesting we make the film guerrilla style. Low budget, skeleton crew. We move fast, we travel light. Get in, get out. Take no prisoners, leave a stack of corpses in our wake. All for under eight hundred grand. We peg spring of '95 as the likely production period.

We talk about *Roadkill* and *61*, what Bruce was doing with those films, and what he hopes to do differently with this one. The main difference is that this one will be about an actual touring rock band. Bruce had actually planned for *Roadkill* to be a documentary about a real band on tour, but the band in question broke up shortly before filming was to begin, so Don McKellar wrote a feature script and they filmed that instead. *Roadkill* is still Bruce's best film. It's everything a low budget independent film should be: rough, funny, irreverent, energetic, and smart. We discuss our desire to make *Hard Core Logo* the definitive Canadian rock 'n' roll movie.

And the coolest movie ever made about Vancouver.

Produced by a bunch of guys from Toronto.

29 August 1994

Signed my contract, pocketed some advance money. Screenwriter contracts are horrifying documents. You assign all rights to others. I mean all rights, full ownership of characters, lines, and ideas. Full ownership of your dreams. Not a problem in this case, as you've merely been hired to re-dream Michael Turner's dreams. Still, the contract lets you know where you the writer stand in brutally frank legal language. You can be fired at any time. You are powerless and for the most part anonymous, unless you also happen to direct, produce, and/or act. Your credit can be taken away from you. Once your work is bought, it's like a house you've designed and sold. The new owners can do whatever they want to it, add mock-Tudor beams, Disneyland castle turrets, plastic fountains, pink flamingoes, garden gnomes, things that satisfy desires and contingencies that have nothing at all to do with you and your original intent for your material. Naturally you love the work, you've been dying for this opportunity, but you basically agree to let people rape you in perpetuity while waiving your right to complain about it. You are consoled by the thought that a movie could get made here, clearing the way for a long career of much more lucrative rapes.

The waiting begins on *Hard Core,* as Brian and Bruce put together a development budget to submit along with the treatment to Telefilm Canada and the Ontario Film Development Corporation (OFDC). I turn my attention back to other projects, projects over which David Griffith and I exercise complete control and dominion (since hardly anyone has seen them).

6 September 1994

Siobhan has brought home a beagle puppy. We're calling her Scout. She's quickly fallen into the habit (Scout, that is) of parking herself on my feet as I write. We all live in a studio apartment atop a medical office building on College Street. I spend way more time than is healthy facing one wall, tapping things into my computer. Occasionally Scout lifts herself, stumbles around on baby legs, takes a leak on the wall-to-wall plastic we've taped down, then falls in it. Siobhan divides her time between the apartment, the university (she's one of the damned, working on her Ph.D. in English), and various cool clubs where she DJs by night, making the lion's share of the money that keeps the Puppy Chow coming and this roof over our heads. People tell me that where puppies enter a household, babies are sure to follow. We shall see.

11 September 1994

The Toronto International Film Festival is underway. They screen one shitload of films to justify all these parties. I'm obviously getting some mileage out of being "the guy who's writing Bruce McDonald's next picture," as the party invites attest. Some local industry people are aware of the project already. Bruce has been dropping hints about it in all the press he's been doing for the premiere of *Dance Me Outside*.

Beautiful Sunday afternoon. Siobhan and I arrive at the Sutton Place Hotel (the film festival HQ) to wait for a special bus that will whisk invitees to the bucolic uptown acreage of the Canadian Film Centre on Bayview for their annual film festival barbecue. Been looking forward to this one.

The Canadian Film Centre was founded back in '87 or '88 by the director Norman Jewison. The gracious estate the Film Centre calls home was donated by a wealthy horseman named E.P. Taylor. The aim of the place is to help working directors, writers, and producers punch up their skills in narrative filmmaking. Many people think of the Film Centre barbecue as *the* festival party, the place where all the heavyweights — American, European, Canadian — show up at once. As we wait around in the lobby, we spot Vanessa Redgrave, looking lean and aristocratic, here to promote the film *Little Odessa*. Finally the bus arrives and we (that is Siobhan, me, and fifty non-famous others) squeeze our way on. After a crowded half-hour ride we are waved through a set of gates past a pair of svelte babes with clipboards. The hard core shmoozers fight their way off the bus and pour through the front door to the manse, eager to make every second count. We finally get through the doors, take a left, veer right, head for the back terrace. Step out the door into an anxious crush of linen-clad Film Types, and Siobhan and I are quickly separated. I am propelled forward by the eager ones behind, and bump straight into this black chick with dreads.

'Scuse me honey, she says, turning around. Stop in my tracks, catch my breath, nod, squeak out some dashing riposte along the lines of "Aiiiieeesssorra." Whoopi Goldberg gives me a weird look, nods back, returns to her conversation with Norman Jewison. I step around them and scan the grounds for the nearest bar as Siobhan joins some friends.

Tend to feel buck naked at these confabs without a drink in hand. I bet most of the writers do in the midst of all these professional extroverts. Then again, I hardly know any real writers in this director-driven government-sponsored film industry which hands most of the feature film cash to a cadre of young auteurs who tend, for better or (all too often) worse, to write all their own scripts. Then again, a closer look reveals writers all over the place. They're the ones huddled in unemotive little groups like nerds at the school dance while the cool kids unself-consciously party their asses off.

Spot a bar out on the lawn to the right. Deke around this bearded red-haired tattered rubbie who turns out to be Eric Stoltz, squeeze past a wildly giggling young woman who looks uncannily like Meg Tilly (big surprise: she is), get stuck in a bottleneck behind Roger Ebert who is just now chewing the fat with someone who I'm pretty sure is John Frankenheimer.

The men part, I spot my opening, zip through. Get in the bar lineup. Get my beer. Guzzle it. Get another one, guzzle it. Get another one, take a genteel sip. Now I can relax.

Go look for more people I recognize, and who also happen to recognize me back. Turns out to be a humblingly tall order, but at last I latch on to a couple of writer residents from the Film Centre. Excellent unproduced writers, also struggling to have careers in our director-driven film culture. They've heard I'm writing Bruce's next picture, and they covet my good fortune to be working with one of the few major Canadian directors who knows what screenwriters are for. Discussion about how in this land of brutally limited opportunity, this kind of project is paydirt. I bask in their envy for a while and split just before it turns into resentment and hatred.

Time to keep cruising. Gotta work the lawn. Gotta meet people. It's festival time, and people have festival fever. Everywhere you look people are talking deals. Everywhere is the F-word: funding. How to get it, how to spend it. Everywhere necks are craning and heads are looking over shoulders. Looking for fresh blood, someone more famous, more influential, closer to the money. Whole lawn's covered with stalkers.

Strike up a conversation with this sharp-eyed, slightly seedy-looking Brit who turns out to be a development guy with the British Film Institute. For some reason I can't talk to him like a civilized human being, I have to go and pitch him this slasher picture idea David Griffith and I knocked together about a guy named Petrus who's so obsessed with the woman he loves that he cuts off the feet of anyone who gets too close to her. The BFI guy is just staring like he's waiting for the punchline. He can't tell if I'm taking the piss, or if I've maybe mistaken him for Roger Corman. The BFI is art film: Derek Jarman, Peter Greenaway, Peter Wollen. People like that. I can see that this is the wrong story, the wrong audience, the wrong time, the wrong place. Still I babble on (it's the fever), all the while thinking, just stop, just shut the fuck up, cut your losses. Can't help it though. It keeps coming, all the way to the end where Petrus is basically disemboweled on a frozen lake by the woman he loves. Stand there grinning. The BFI guy stares at me like I'm a strain of ebola just breaking out. Feeling one power of a thirst, I put beer bottle to lips, throw head back, open throat, and let contents empty into me. Okay, I say, maybe it's not a story that has to be told. The BFI guy is gracious enough as he cuts and runs to say, But it's a story that *might* be told. Still puzzling over that one.

I take refuge with Brian Dennis who tells me Bruce is out of town prepping an episode of some TV series called *Taking the Falls*. Seen the briefs on this one and it looks abysmal. A well-known Canadian TV actress plays a private eye in Niagara Falls. Lite mystery, intrigue, romance in a touristy border town. Meaning there'll be some clichéd American bad guys up to no good on our fair soil. Makes a strange kind of sense for TV in this country, since there's no such thing as a clichéd Canadian bad guy. (I feel a rant coming on.) Our real bad guys, our newsworthy criminals, are the likes of Paul Bernardo, Clifford Olson, Marc Lepine. We're not even really talking bad guys here, we're talking off-the-scale fucking *psychos*. Put the likes of these guys on in prime time and Canadian TV would sure as hell be a lot less boring, a lot less cliché-riven. Of course our shows could always try to do away with clichés altogether and strive for originality . . . Nah. It's government funded "drama." Can't do it. Can't afford to take any risks. Bets must be hedged wherever possible.

Typical Canadian TV producer's ploy: get taxpayer bucks to develop a series that will be Canadian enough for the government regulators, but more important, American enough to grab that big brass ring, a U.S. network or cable sale. Lightning struck once up here with *Due South*, because the Mountie-in-America shtick is the one Canadian cliché that Americans actually get. What will it take for lightning to strike again? How about comedy that's actually funny. Drama that's actually absorbing. You always read these Canadian producers moaning in the papers that TV is so expensive to produce, you have to develop a series with your eyes wide open, planning the American sale from day one. Canadian TV is rationalized into mediocrity year in and year out because producers think they have to compete with U.S. production values. They're so wrong. The only place they have to compete is in the quality of concept, character, and drama. I'm all for cheap and strong. As is Bruce. We've agreed that *HCL*, whatever its lowly government-funded budget (probably on par with an episode of *Taking the Falls*), is going to rock right down to the soles of its Canadian-made stompin' boots.

15 September 1994

Other festival parties: one at the Bovine Sex Club (Siobhan's the DJ here) for a low-bud film I can't remember the name of and didn't see. The place is jammed from end to end. Shoulder my way through a sweating clusterfuck of hipsters and end up at the bar next to, of all people, John Cusack. Long, awkward wait for drinks. Must've been staring at him, 'cause he sticks out his hand, a friendly smile. I'm Johnny, he says. Says he's here for the premiere of *Bullets Over Broadway*, then asks what my story is. A very short one it turns out, as my brain suddenly enters a state of no-mind that would do a Zen master proud. Then a more animated being squeezes between us and that's that. At least I've progressed to handshakes and how are yas in these brushes with fame. Some day conversation will follow and I will be whole.

Alliance party at the Royal Ontario Museum. A more upmarket guest list than most of the other bashes. This one's clearly for the suits, but that doesn't stop them from jostling to get their fill of the free Jamie Kennedy food just like the few down-at-the-heels filmmakers who've crashed it. Everyone seems to want the lobster, as the hundred-person-long queue attests. Expensively dressed people are lining up, getting their lobster, and immediately rejoining the queue as they eat the lobster they've already got, the trick being to polish it off just as they reach the front again. The lobster is definitely the life of this party.

OFDC (Ontario Film Development Corporation) party at the top of the CN tower. No stars way up here in the sky, just the business people, bureaucrats, and a battery of ever-thirsty gatecrashing writers and directors. This being a government-sponsored event, the word "funding" (not "investment" or "financing") floats on the air all night, thick as the vile cigar smoke blowing from the mouths of all the lemmings who've heard that cigar smoking is way cool now. Have to smoke one cigarette after another to mask the smell around me.

All this partying. Try to convince myself that I have to go to these events, get out there, get a grip on this networking thing, promote myself. I return home night after night, my wallet loaded with the business cards of Italian film critics, Swiss commissioning editors, South American distributors, German television programmers, Mexican directors, Canadian Film Centre students. The cards I really want but never get are those belonging to agents from CAA, ICM, William Morris.

18 September 1994

Ten days and nights of canapés, garlicky veggie dips, and complimentary booze. Haven't had a real meal the whole time the festival was on. Haven't seen the Bruce-man either. He's still working away in Niagara Falls. I'm completely bagged from all this hanging out. Serious case of schmooze-poisoning that could take weeks to sweat out of my system. Made it to only one film. One film? Last year it was ten days and nights of popcorn and coffee as I paced myself through a thirty film marathon. How priorities can change in a year.

Thinking about actually getting down to writing the first draft of *HCL*. Waiting to see what Telefilm and the OFDC think of the treatment first. In the Canadian film business, many if not most projects begin when a writer-director-producer team (or writer/director-producer team) submits a twenty page treatment for a feature script to the agencies (as Telefilm and its provincial counterparts are known) for development funding.

The material is vetted by the on-staff development officers as well as outside freelance readers (I've been one of these for both agencies the last couple of years), who submit reader's reports evaluating its potential. If you get the nod after the usual two month wait for a response, cheques are eventually issued for script development, at which point your project is officially on the agenda and you, the writer (or writer/director) part of the team, can forge ahead secure in the knowledge that even if the film is never made, you are getting paid to write.

All scripts developed with Telefilm money are assigned a story editor whose job is to offer ongoing advice and feedback to the writer. Eventually, when you and the rest of your team are confident that your polished script is ready to be submitted for all the marbles — production funding — it goes in along with the producer's budget and letters of interest from Canadian distributors and/or broadcasters.

The whole package is then evaluated. More readers' reports are generated. If you get the nod at that point, guess what? You're making a Canadian movie! Yeehaa!

And if it's successful outside the country (rare, but it's been known to happen), you might just get to do your next one

Stateside for a hell of a lot more money. Not everyone working here wants this, but let's face it: many do.

As for *HCL*, it's a bit premature to speculate about its chances. I'm going to assume we'll get past the first hurdle and qualify for development financing. What is frustrating is how long it takes merely to get to the first hurdle. It's like I've been "sort of hired" but I'm still essentially writing on spec. Brian tells me the agencies won't be reviewing our application for a couple of weeks, so it'll be a while yet before my first real payday comes.

We won't be letting you starve, he says.

4 October 1994

Two solid weeks of work. I look up to see that I've written a goodly chunk of the first draft. Won't be surprised if it's done in another week. So far it's mostly a bulked out version of the treatment with added visual detail and scenes fleshed out with more beats. I love this material and hope I can bring the book's sensibility straight to the screen without having to get too much in the way. This is nothing to do with laziness, but a desire to see the best aspects of the book reach the screen as the author intended. This is just a first draft, though, and changes will be coming down the road.

Bruce checks in by phone from time to time. He's around, doing whatever he does at his office. Stuff to do with *Dance*. Stuff to do with the TV series they're developing from it. Stuff to do with this script he has called *Yummy Fur*, based on Chester Brown's bizarre 1980s underground comic about Ed the Happy Clown. In Bruce's heart of hearts, *Yummy Fur* is the film he yearns most to make. Flipped through the press kit and comic book at Bruce's office recently. It's a fabulous, completely insane movie idea but very difficult to sell. There's a character called "The Man Who Couldn't Stop Shitting" whose anus is a portal to another dimension, and a clown (i.e., Ed the Happy) who wakes up one day to find that the head of his penis has transformed into Ronald Reagan's head. Obviously the president belongs in the other dimension, not in the clown's pants. To fix the dimensional rift, there is but one solution, and that is for the happy clown to insert his penis into the anus of the man who couldn't stop shitting and send the president home.

Well jeez, no wonder it's a hard sell. Reagan on the head of a penis? Totally dated.

8 October 1994

Meeting a few days ago with the development people at the Ontario Film Development Corporation. Their offices are at the corner of Bloor and Church, heart of the Insurance District. I love the OFDC; they've supported my stuff for about four years via their Screenwriter Program, which gives money to promising writers with promising scripts. By now they must be hoping like hell I'm going to deliver on this promise, justify their investment. It's a great comfort to come into these offices tied by a magic thread to a viable director-producer team. Makes everything seem so much more concrete, so much closer to becoming a reality.

Bruce, Brian, and I talk over the treatment with development officers Marlene Rogers and David Weaver, who both seem very interested in seeing something happen with this one. David in particular has done some homework and wants to know how we're going to handle this material. What's the angle: mockumentary? Straight drama in a verité style? Maybe something much more stylized? Bruce says that whatever the movie ends up looking like, it's gonna be cool. I back that up all the way. Brian talks about the numbers. Then we're out of there. On the way back to the office I ask Brian if things are going as well at Telefilm. Have they said anything about the treatment, does he have any sense of where they stand? He seems less confident about them.

15 October 1994

Pitch meeting at Telefilm today, wherein we justify our application for development funding for the first draft of the script. Which I've already almost finished writing, but we won't tell them this.

Bruce, Brian, and I arrive at Telefilm's plush offices high above the corner of Bloor and Yonge. The nerve center of English Canadian cinema. We're led to a boardroom and asked to wait. Glorious sunshine outside. There's an impressive wall-to-wall view of downtown Toronto and Lake Ontario to the south. The boardroom table is a thirty foot tongue of blonde ash. Federal cabinet meetings could take place here with seats to spare. We wait and wait some more. Bruce is cool and relaxed. He's done this before. Brian and I chatter casually. The fact that I've been a reader for this agency and know a little bit about the way film treatments are evaluated does little to quell my anxiety. It's the first time I've been through this door to ask for money. I wipe my palms on my pants fifty or sixty times.

Finally Michelle McLean enters. She's the manager of things creative at Telefilm. With her is a fellow named John who carries a lined yellow pad and a pencil. We all sit at one end of the monster table, with John sitting a few seats off jotting notes. The usual small talk (okay, like I know what's "usual"), then it's down to business. Michelle is briskly professional, pleasant, and polite. She's read the treatment and she's "intrigued," but her body language hints at a distinct lack of excitement.

Brian weighs in first from our side, talking about the business end: budget, the market, and so on. Bruce says he wants to make the movie because it's about a band on the road; it's what he would have done with *Roadkill* had things gone his way five years ago.

Then my turn comes and I pitch the story, explaining themes, structure, and so on. Michelle listens politely. Then comes the feared response: without spelling it out too clearly, she implies that Telefilm thinks Bruce should move on with his career and not do another road movie right now. And then Bruce, also without spelling it out too clearly, basically says tough shit, I'm doing this movie anyway. Things start to chill down in the room. I want to ask why Telefilm has no trouble funding filmmakers who specialize, film in and film out, in, say, lesbian love stories or frigid parables about contemporary alienation, yet they have such a problem funding Bruce within his area of interest. Naturally I keep my mouth shut. Things end inconclusively. Smiles and handshakes, then we leave.

On the street Brian and I start analyzing every second of the meeting, every gesture, every phrase. What did she mean when she said . . . etc. Bruce isn't worried. It's all a dance, he says. He assures me the development money's coming and wants me to finish the first draft ASAP. He's totally confident that we'll make the movie. I'm not even confident I'll make my rent.

26 October 1994

The words are flowing like cold roofing pitch. This draft has proved more difficult than I thought. It's much more than a process of bulking out the treatment into a string of snappy scenes. Though this is largely what I've done, and many of these scenes are, I think, pretty good. The problem is structural, even though the road story provides a concrete site for a journey you might describe as mythic. I've taken Turner's book and transcribed it, and I now see that it reads like a book in script form and has yet to take on a life of its own as a movie script. Have to figure out how to make these characters work for film. Have to ask myself smarter questions about them. Have to go over the script a few more times before I can call the draft finished.

*

So what is it with Joe Dick, who will be almost thirty-five by the time we make this film? Clinging so hard to these punk ideals that he adopted at age seventeen, half a lifetime ago. The band's tour seems like a final test for Joe's late-70s West Coast punk values, a test he fails along with the band. But a test that transforms him into a realist, an adult.

What happens to him after the story ends? I suspect he'll retain his propensity to shock, to reject authority, to prod and satirize, scream with rage, champion the underdog, etc. What he won't do is continue to bite the hand that feeds him. If he does, they'll be love bites. He'll play by the rules of the business, and this is in many ways the ultimate capitulation for an old punk. Rock 'n' roll is a business where coming of age largely means playing by established rules, being a part of the system. Selling out.

———————— who the hell do you think you are? ————————

*

What is it with punk these days, anyway? Everywhere you go in Toronto, there are these armies of punks with squeegees on street corners, washing windshields when cars stop for red lights. How the hell did this become, specifically, a punk franchise? You see them at Bathurst and College, Spadina and Queen. Green mohawks, tattered army pants, pierced bodies, ready-made extras for post-apocalyptic B-movies. There was a time when punks, like Hard Core Logo and their fans, thrived on the illusion that they were defying the status quo, that their dissent was meaningful in the wider world. Obviously, the impetus for defiance is gone. The fashions remain, but they're mere emblems of solidarity among those who've opted to apply entrepreneurial principles to surviving the street. The political sting is gone, the dissenters are bought off with a few coins grudgingly handed over by obliging Canadian drivers.

10 November 1994

Solid jam on *HCL* the last week. Closing in on the draft. It goes well.

19 November 1994

Finished. In spite of several new scenes invented and many excisions of book material, the script still hews closely to Turner's intentions. I think I've hit the right balance between the book's lyricism and the cinematic demand for vivid pictures and plenty of narrative forward-thrust.

The script retains some dialogue from the book, especially Joe Dick's interviews with alternative press and college radio journalists. Bucky Haight's monologue makes the transit largely intact, though it takes up a full eight pages. Much as I like it, it'll probably be one of the first things to shrink in the next draft, as it is likely to soak up eight to ten minutes of screen time, an eternity in film. All the rest is adapted from scenes suggested by the book. I've jacked up the drama at the climax and the script ends well, I think, with Joe and Billy having a huge fist-fight on stage during the final performance of the band's tour. The personal becomes public and the band is destroyed for good. It's not a happy ending, but it's a true ending. I've done the best I can do at this stage. Now I wait for feedback.

24 November 1994

Friends of mine have read the draft and it gets several thumbs up.

Then comes my first script meeting with Bruce and Brian. The consensus: well done boyo, not bad for a first draft, but too dialogue-driven, an unending talkfest, needs to be transformed into something far more visual. Could stand to be paced a tad faster too. Bruce has a number of visual ideas for the film. I wanted to preserve some of the book's chapter headings as textual markers in the film (as in "Ladies and Gentlemen, Joe Dick . . ." and "Bucky Got Drunk, Told Stories," and so on). Bruce suggests we do some wacky animation effects along with the text bumpers to make it look snappier. I'm not so sure about this myself. I see this as a verité style film and fear that visual gimmicks are going to compromise something that should succeed on dramatic merits alone. Simple text on black screen will be clean and classy. I tell Bruce that I'm very inspired by Woody Allen's *Husbands and Wives*, shot mostly off the shoulder. There are moments, as in *HCL*, where the characters simply sit in

──────── who the hell do you think you are ? ────────

front of the camera and speak candidly, as if they're being interviewed by someone they trust.

*

Me, rewriting already, left.
Brian Dennis talking to the money, right.

Leaving the office at the end of the day with Brian, a black Saab Turbo pulls up at the door. Tinted window rolls down to reveal a greying bundle of nervous energy, Norman Jewison. Brian starts up a conversation with him. Norman sits in his car, talking a mile a minute about *Dance Me Outside* business (Norman's the executive producer). Finally a break in this pinball conversation and Brian introduces me to him. Norman is immediately interested. You a writer? Great! Hey, writers are the lifeblood! Nice to meet ya! Whatcha working on, *Yummy Fur*? No? What then? *Hard Core Logo*? What's that? Oh yeah, new thing, huh? Well that's just great! See ya around!

So this is the Norman I've been hearing about all this time. Leaves you wishing that a few more of the Canadians with A-list careers in L.A. showed a shred of this kind of encouragement to the younger talent back home.

15 December 1994

Moved into a new place a couple of weeks ago. I hate it. What were we thinking? This place is a dump. The idea was to find a house with a yard for the dog, and a spare room for me to work in, one of those home office tax write-off deals. We found one without looking all that hard, about two blocks from the old apartment. Rent was reasonable by Toronto standards, seemed like a good deal at the time.

Haven't looked at the script once, as I spent two whole weeks repainting the walls and one floor to give this place the faintest illusion of livability. Then we noticed our mistake. The neighbors have two dogs who don't seem to like Scout much, and whose shit lies ankle deep on their patio. If it wasn't so cold it'd be a health hazard out there. Half the parquet on our bedroom floor is coming up thanks to water damage. Scout has chewed most of the loose pieces beyond repair. It now smells like creeping death down here. Yeah, down here. Where I'd hoped to work, in a "spare" room in the basement. My "study." Went to town doing up the walls in many layers of dark green wash. Laid carpet. Lined the room with bookshelves. Et voila, instant lair of a bourgeois gentilhomme.

Then came the rains, evidence of leakage, the flood in the night, the damp rot, the smell, and once again it's a disgusting little crypt where nobody but an idiot or a Goth would ever want to spend his working days. There's no window, no fresh air. I move my desk and computer up to the living room and discover that it gets dark out at something like four o'clock anyway. My body thinks it's bedtime twenty hours a day. I should be working on the second draft, but just don't have the energy to deal with Joe and Billy and John and Pipe, and anyway, my five-year-old computer screen keeps crapping out. The news is filled with the triumphs of other writers and filmmakers at the Genie Awards, people who probably work in nice, bright, dry, spacious rooms.

19 December 1994

First casting session at Shadow Shows. This is exciting. I've been to lots of other peoples' casting sessions, never one for a script of my own.

We see about forty actors, reading for the four leads. As I watch the hopefuls go through this agonizing process, I realize that writers know something about pressure and rejection, but actors feel it in a far more immediate way. All day these actors come in, most of whom probably spent a day or two getting their lengthy monologues down. Many of them are also musicians and they let us know that they've really "connected" with their characters, that they were born for these roles. Some are serious theater actors who tend to linger over their dialogue, to make slow and painful love to it. On the whole, the actors who impress us the most are very offhand in their readings, as if they just don't give a shit about anything.

For some reason, a lot of the guys our casting director has sent us are tattooed tough guy types. Some of them think that because the band members are punk rockers, they must also be boneheaded subhuman freaks, and they skew their performances accordingly. Our casting director and these actors must be thinking of the typical Hollywood misrepresentation of punk as a moronic and mindlessly violent subculture. Whereas we're thinking of the cool, highly ironic, witty, gleeful, irreverent expression of consumer and class anger that punk was. Punks like the Pistols, the Clash, Dead Kennedys, and X, were all highly intelligent, politically sophisticated, and in their own ways funny. Today's talent pool just does not get it.

Scratch that. One actor gets it, but he's reading for the role of Bucky Haight. He is Julian Richings, born British, mid-thirties, based in Toronto. He looks the part: gaunt, his narrow face all cheekbone and wide eyes, his body wiry like a junkie's. Then there's his skill: he performs the entire eight pages of the monologue without once looking at the script. It takes him over ten minutes, but he nails every single line, stressing all the right words, hitting all the right nuances, sounding like an old junkie describing the indignities, out-

Julian Richings, getting it.

rages, and humiliations of his life with just enough wry detachment for them to sound utterly chilling, the antithesis of the polished and oft-told Showbiz Anecdote. This guy's the shit.

3 January 1995

We do a read-through of the script at the office with actors. Justin Louis reads for Joe, Paul Ekniss, a rock guitarist and former Nina Hagen boyfriend, reads for Billy, Joel Bissonette reads for John, and another musician friend of Bruce's, Robbie Rox, reads for Pipefitter. Julian does Bucky. I read the interviewers and bit parts. We go through the whole script in the morning and I pay attention to what works, what doesn't. In the afternoon, the people from Telefilm and the OFDC are coming to watch a slightly more polished read-through, but first we break for lunch. On the way to the restaurant Justin falls in next to me and asks how he's faring as Joe Dick. I tell him the thing I've liked about him so far is the way he nonchalantly mumbles his lines like he doesn't give a fuck, yet still gets the edge and attitude across. He nods and sort of files this away.

The afternoon reading with the agency people present goes better than this morning's, for the most part. The actors generally hit their lines harder and with greater understanding. Except for Justin, who mumbles most of his lines almost unintelligibly. I can see Bruce looking at him funny.

After the reading and the departure of the agency people and actors, Bruce, Brian, Sandy, and I sit around discussing how it went. Great, it seemed to go over relatively well. What about the actors though, what about Justin as Joe Dick? Bruce says he thinks Justin's an okay cat, but what was all that mumbling about? Next!

Screenwriter lesson #79: Don't talk to the actors in rehearsal, your enthusiasms may sabotage their chances.

4 January 1995
Stuff I learned about Bruce in 1994.

He has an infinite capacity to keep people interested in his projects. Understands the importance of giving a project an image and identity long before it is ready for production, as this goes a long way to creating momentum. He's joked that the real reason he makes movies is to have cool movie posters with his name on them. He calls the rock 'n' roll persona he maintains "a dog and pony show."

He usually wears jeans, army boots and untucked shirts, sometimes a bandanna wrapped over his head, but maybe twice a month he has this other look: beige chinos, a truly conservative shirt, tortoiseshell glasses, the unaffected, studious film nerd. I suspect this is who Bruce really is when the dogs and ponies have gone home.

He loves Bob Dylan.

He loves his girlfriend and his voice becomes extra tender when he speaks with her on the phone.

He always picks up the cheque.

He's kept up a friendship with Joey Ramone since *Roadkill*. Joey sent Bruce a Christmas card a couple of weeks ago, which sits on his desk. Picture of Santa turning around from filling stockings to discover he's being watched by a little boy. Santa says something like, "Merry Xmas, Timmy. Of course now you've seen me, I'm going to have to kill you." If Bruce had it his way, he'd personally know far more rock stars. He wants to direct the coolest film ever made.

I still don't know what his favorite film is.

2.

LAKE ONTARIO SMELLS LIKE SHIT

7 January 1995, Vancouver

Bruce and I are here to do some casting, check out locations, soak up local flavor for the script.

The city is hiding out under cloud as the plane descends and the vaunted mountains are nowhere to be seen. Bruce has never been here before. I did much of my growing up here. Of all the places I lived as a kid — California, Michigan, France, Southern Ontario, Vancouver — it is Vancouver that I think of as my home town. My mother lives here. I have aunts, uncles, cousins, and grandmothers out here. Many of my most intense, lifelong friendships were forged here, and many friends are still around. They tend to hate Toronto. Even the ones who've never been there. I left here for Toronto at the end of 1986, which to many Vancouverites is not just a move but a sort of urban infidelity, a betrayal that defies erotic logic. Leaving Vancouver for Toronto is like leaving Princess Di for Camilla Parker-Bowles.

We book into the Sylvia, a lovely old fleabag on English Bay. The air is refreshingly mild, a relief from the kick-in-the-balls cold we left behind in Toronto. First on the agenda is a party at Keith Porteous's place in Chinatown where we're supposed to meet Michael Turner and Douglas Coupland. We meet Turner anyway, Coupland having been whisked off unexpectedly to Japan or somewhere to flog his current gazillion-selling take on whatever technosocial fever or malaise is supposedly gripping young America this year. We've been looking forward to meeting Turner, but Keith says that Turner has apprehensions about meeting us. We're movie guys, we come from a different place, work in a different medium. Does he really want to meet the cretins who are going to butcher his story?

Long after I've been fully convinced that Turner has given the soirée a miss, he strides in with his friends. He wears a red checked mac, black jeans, his hair slicked back. Intelligent dark eyes, ironic smile. He has the elocution of a literary man, takes care to pronounce all his consonants. His sense of humor has an edge. He teases people. He's friendly but wary of us. Fortunately Bruce radiates warmth, so the ice soon cracks and we're all talking about the project. Keith stands by grinning, the impresario who brought us all together. We all seem to like each other even more after smoking a joint. Then it's suddenly four in the morning, seven for the Toronto guys. We agree to meet for dinner tomorrow night.

*

Someone brought these questionnaires to the party, which are to be filled out and sealed in a time capsule for a year, when they will be read aloud at next year's version of this very party.* There are many personal questions and I answer most of them glibly, fearing that excess earnestness will bore next year's guests. I look over Bruce's shoulder as he fills his questionnaire out. In answer to the question, *What do you fear most?* he has written *Being found out.* I know the feeling well.

---

* I never do learn the fate of the questionnaire. Keith moved to Toronto a few months later and I never saw his party guests again.

8 January 1995

Hangovers from hell. Pissing rain. Bruce and I cruise around town checking locations, talking about the project, listening to a sampler of the old Vancouver punk scene on the car stereo. Forty-eight songs from the golden years. Bruce has never heard this stuff, though for me it's a music-of-yer-life compilation, all familiar stuff from my college radio days here.

We cruise around Hastings and Main a fair bit. Junkies, drunks, the homeless, natives, people punching the air, people on the verge of puking their guts out. Old neon, rooming houses, sleazy hotels, discount stores, pawn shops. The only block in Vancouver that hasn't changed in fifty years. Bruce makes little drawings in his notebook, snaps pictures. I take notes. The director and writer at work in their own ways. Somewhere along the way I float up a balloon about turning my diary notes into a book on the production of the movie, opportunism being second nature for screenwriters. Bruce says "go for it." So now it seems that these notes are intended for an audience. So much for the narrative fourth wall.

After a hard day's cruising we stop for a beer at the old American Hotel on Main, the biker bar where Hard Core Logo played their first ever gig in Turner's book (and, so far, in the script). This is what they used to call a beer parlor out here, an old style hotel bar, a vintage low-rent dive, with bartenders who look like they've done stretches of hard time. Kind of bar where you wipe your feet as you leave.

There's a table of old coots checking us out as we drink draft at a table covered with a sort of terry cloth diaper. A young loogan walks in looking like he's just breezed through a time portal from 1973. He's joined by another of his ilk. Two guys caught in a nasty time warp. That's loogan culture for you. People who know every word to every song Nazareth ever recorded. Long feathered hair, parted in the middle. Tattoos. Muscles tensed for the next fight. No wonder Joe Dick and the boys were shit-scared first time they played here.

Air's always vibrating with the potential for violence in places like this, and four young punk rockers would be all too aware of their vulnerability in a piss-up joint with a long established and fairly rigid loogan code. It's never ceased to amaze me that a haircut is all the provocation it takes to get you beaten up or maybe even killed. Haircuts are potentially dangerous vanities. The brain's own clothing, as it were, broadcasting your attitude to the world. At least this is how it was in the late 70s before MTV sent tribal styles mainstream and made weirdness safer for the masses. Our haircuts provoke no hostility from the denizens. We take some pictures, drink up, and split.

We meet Keith and Turner for dinner in the West End. Martinis are ordered. Talk about the project at last. Turner is very hands-off, resisting the temptation to say what he'd "like to see done" with his story on screen. I'm still feeling odd, maybe even guilty, about my position as adapter of his work. Until this project came along, I did only original work. Now it's like I'm rooting around in this guy's closet, hauling out the items of clothing I want to steal, taking them to a tailor for alterations. I feel compelled to explain what I'm up to. I tell Turner I see the book as a sort of elegiac romance, a lament for the end of the powerful adolescent relationship between Joe and Billy. He agrees and warms to us, this literary terminology allaying his fear that movie morons are about to fuck up his work.

Encouraged, I move on to compare *HCL* to books and films that ritualize male bonding against a backdrop of mythic journeying. The work of Cormack McCarthy, especially *All The Pretty Horses* and *Blood Meridian*. James Dickey's *Deliverance*. *Apocalypse Now*. It's not like I've been trying to flatter him so much as prove that I am up to the task of doing right by his book. I want to prove that I understand its themes. Why this need to prove anything? The guy sold his film rights, we can do what we want with the story. Yet my need for the author's approval or friendship remains. Do other screenwriters feel like this when they're adapting books? I'm aware of needing the approval of the director, producer, and funding bodies, as in getting the script "approved" for production, but this is a practical, political need, not a personal one. Such vanity — not only in wanting the work to measure up to the original creation, but in the desire to measure up to the original creator.

We move on to the Town Pump and catch the end of a Wool concert. Afterwards we hang out and drink. Keith introduces us to a tattooed, black-haired female rocker named Biff Naked. She talks very tough, casts a cold assessing eye on everything and everyone around her, including us. The bar closes and we all repair to Keith's to drink up whatever booze is left after last night. Turner picks up a guitar and plays "The Big Bush Party After School," a cheesy campfire song Hard Core Logo sing in their van on tour. It's the first Hard Core Logo music we've heard, and it's coming right from the poet's mouth. A downright catchy tune. Soon we all join in and we're belting it out like a chorus of Hank Snows. Keith's roommate comes downstairs in her nightgown and she's livid. It's four in the morning yet again and she's got a class in a few hours. She boots us out.

9 January 1995

Hangovers from hell again. Steady rain again. Casting session at this plush building on Granville Island. We must just reek of last night's booze as we take position behind a table in a small, windowless, airless room.

The talent is led in at the usual twenty minute intervals. Same protocols in effect as in Toronto: in they come, brisk introductions. Some of them crack jokes they've probably been practicing for just this moment, the crucial first-impression window, before the reading kicks in. A little chitchat with Bruce, who as usual asks them what they've been up to. Out here the answers are different: most of them have been up to TV work on some fairly major shows. We see guys who've guested on the *X-Files* and other American series shot here. These guys are camera ready and in general much more polished and natural screen actors than the talent pool in Toronto.

We see seasoned pros, excellent actors who are too young or too old, some who bring their guitars, some who are definitely interesting but not quite what we want, some who are a bit too slick, too polished. Some utter freaks. One or two assholes. For instance, one haughty but quite strikingly handsome bald guy comes in to audition for Billy, and Bruce has me read with him through the Edmonton interview scene. I run through the questions off the page, expecting the actor to have Billy's responses memorized. But the bald guy explains that he doesn't believe in the tyranny of printed words (or some such horseshit), and as he apparently hasn't bothered to learn the lines, he improvises. We are quickly lost. He gets impatient with my stubborn fidelity to the text and suggests I "loosen up a bit" and just "make some shit up." I detect a manic glint in his eyes. I look at Bruce.

Bruce looks at the maniac. The maniac glares at me. Standoff. Bruce helpfully offers the guy some sides to sight-read. Guy snatches them and reads his way angrily through his part, fucking up from end to end. Then he turns on us like it's our fault, offers some cutting insults about the project, storms out, pausing to snidely invite us down to some club where he go-go dances on a box for a living, should we want to see "some real rock 'n' roll" while we're in town. Yeesh.

I propose a short film starring all the bald psychos we've seen for this film, called *Scary Fuckin Bald Guys*. It would consist of interviews about what pisses these guys off, intercut with answers to questions about their mothers. Could be your directing début, says Bruce.

Another guy who looks about forty swaggers in got up like Sid Vicious circa '77. (It's a punk rock movie, right?) He explains that his wife helped him with his punker costume the previous night. There are safety pins everywhere, his hair is jet-black and standing on end, he grunts a fair bit and throws as much attitude as he can muster. Our first impression is Next!, but you've got to let everyone read. So "Sid" does Joe while sneering painfully and working up phlegm from the back of his throat. There's even a mangled Cockney accent to drive the cliché home. The reading over, he picks up an acoustic guitar to perform a song he wrote especially for Bruce, a hilarious one-chord rant about being a punker and hating everything in the whole wide world. When we're done laughing and the guy leaves, Bruce drops a big fat X next to his name.

The hours dribble by. The head clears. We've seen several possible callbacks but no one who simply exudes the essence of any of the four band members. Until late in the afternoon, when we finally see an actor who does. Tall, blond, angular,

Seducing the camera: Callum Keith Rennie.

unconventionally handsome, in his thirties. But it's much more than looks that strike us, it's the details of his attitude, his personal style. Unlike all the others he wears brown, not black, and in a way that suggests he knows what he's doing when he opens his closet in the morning. There is no "uniform," and he's not putting on any misconceived punk airs. Quite the opposite. There's something spaced-out and fragile about him, yet also something subtly impertinent and fuck-you in the way he refuses to slate himself properly for the camera. He's got a wicked smile. His name is Callum Rennie, he's reading for Billy, and I know he's our man before he reads a word.

I go through the Edmonton interview scene with him. He's both focused and distanced at the same time, playing Billy's self-absorption with a wholly unexpected, almost damaged, charm. His voice is a shade louder than a whisper, which forces you to lean towards him. This cuts hard against what we've seen from most of our other Billys, who've played him in more aggressively egomaniacal terms. This Billy is going to be one bastard you can love, and one who knows how to seduce the camera. When Rennie leaves, I watch Bruce put a huge tick mark beside his name on the casting sheet. Our casting agent, Wendy O'Brien, tells us that this guy has been on the verge of big things for a while now. I wonder if he knows he nailed it.

Several more Billys come in and Bruce gives them all encouragement and direction in spite of our strong interest in Rennie. We see several more Joes, Johns, and Pipes, but no one who really stands out. Finally we're down to the last actor of the day and we can't wait to get the hell out of here. It's a Pipefitter hopeful who enters wearing a big brown fedora, a short shiny huge-shouldered double-breasted suit jacket that screams 1982, flared slacks and platform shoes. His hair's a shag, dyed popsicle orange with blond roots showing. He's not too tall, has a voice like an outboard in need of oil. We're totally confused and can't tell whether he belongs in the *wrong* category with Sid Vicious, an *original* category with Callum Rennie, or a *freak* category all his own. He could be anywhere from twenty-five to forty years old, hard to tell with rough ones like this. His name is Bernie Coulson.

Bruce sets him up to read a couple of Pipe's long monologues. Bernie stumbles badly, stressing the wrong things, not quite catching the mix of hostility and love that Pipe has towards his bandmates. Bruce stops him, thanks him, asks him what he's been up to lately (meaning he's about to wrap things up and run a line through the name). But there's something about this guy that gets under the skin. I ask Bruce if we can't get Bernie to run through the monologues again, with a bit more coaching. Bruce agrees, explains a few things about Pipefitter.

Oddly lovable: Bernie Coulson.

Bernie runs through the sides again, and this time there's magic. He's got this way of seeming pissed off and funny at the same time, and the fact that he's small makes him much more oddly lovable than so many of the hulking tattooed monsters we've seen for this part. Bruce has him read more, and more. Bernie gets it; he loosens up and improves; we are very impressed. We sit around talking for about half an hour as Bernie tells us about himself (he had a small but key role in *The Accused* with Jodie Foster), finally coming to the clincher: he plays drums. Suddenly we've got two of the leads cast and we're in a mood to celebrate.

Keith suggests we meet for drinks at the Number Five Orange, a legendary Vancouver strip bar where Courtney

———————— lake ontario smells like shit ————————

The original spice girls, Lick the Pole. Rebecca at left.

Love was rumored to have peeled in her pre-rock 'n' roll stripper days. We haul along Chris Dafoe, an old college radio friend who now covers the Western Arts beat for the *Globe and Mail*.

The Five is neon, ultraviolet, candy-colored, halfway surreal, and tonight it's hopping. Bruce and Chris and I squeeze through the overwhelmingly male crowd to a table where Keith is holding court with a bunch of musicians and this strange, sexy, hyperanimated tart named Rebecca, the singer for a campy sleaze-rock band called Lick the Pole. (These women Keith knows!)

Rebecca is the star of the night, magnet for all attention. We hang out for a while, forego the obscenely expensive liquor in favor of four-dollar soda waters, watch strippers, get to know the company. I talk with Rebecca about her deep love for extreme skiing ("going off cliffs is the coolest!"), when suddenly she notices the stage is free. She excuses herself, dances over to the stage, climbs up on it, and starts to grind, slowly unzipping her pants to shimmy out of them. Which is interesting because, as I say to Keith, I didn't know she worked here, and he says, she doesn't. The crowd's whooping. Keith mentions that she might be kinda showing off for Bruce in case he might see fit to put her in the movie.

Later we say good-bye to Keith and give Rebecca a ride to the Railway Club on the way back to our hotel. It's one o'clock and we're bagged. We're still on Toronto time, which really makes it four. But the bars are open til two here, and Rebecca's got hours of partying left in her. Much as we'd like to keep hanging out, we've got to get up and hit the road for Calgary in the morning. We're driving through the mountains to scout locations. So it's goodnight.

Rebecca gets out, takes a step towards the club, then, perhaps concerned that she hadn't made enough of an impression back at the Five, throws herself on the hood and crawls up to the windshield, where to our total amazement she rips her top off and presses her large firm perfect breasts to the glass and more or less howls at the moon. We sit in stunned silence. Or maybe we howl too but just can't hear ourselves. Bruce fumbles in his oversized army jacket for his camera, ever a stickler for documentation. Rebecca gives us one last dazzling smile, slips off the car and disappears into the club. I ask Bruce if I should write her into the picture or what. He shrugs. Maybe she can play Billy's girlfriend.

12 January 1995, Calgary

Hangover from hell yet again. This Bruce guy is clearly a bad influence. Haven't felt so numb after a trip since the time I drove a truckload of art nonstop from New York to Miami with a troglodyte from Jersey City who had lethal BO and a deviated septum.

Bruce and I leave Vancouver and drive up through the cloud-choked mountains, through rain, sleet, finally driving snow, taking location photos. Many, many photos of snow, road, and slate-hued sky. I'd been telling Bruce for weeks about the sheer majesty of this terrain, about the landscape beauty-shot possibilities for the film. But with the charcoal overcast starting at road level we might as well be Hamilton-bound on the QEW in heavy fog. Not the nifty little location scouting holiday we'd hoped for.

Just outside Kamloops a blizzard sets in. In the town of Salmon Arm we buy chains for the rental car at the local Canadian Tire, then decide we'd better stay the night. Place has no strippers, so after a couple pitchers of beer at the only tavern we can find (it's darts night) we settle for watching the latest *Star Trek* movie at the local theater, which is a giant Quonset hut with a street facade and marquee.

Afterwards we compare and contrast the journey of the Enterprise across the galaxy and the journey of Hard Core Logo across Western Canada in their shabby van. The common theme seems to be "you can't go home again." The Enterprise crashes spectacularly onto the surface of some planet at the end, and after a protracted showdown with bad guy Malcolm McDowell, Kirk dies in Picard's arms. What you call a big finish.

Hard Core Logo is, let's face it, a little more subdued at the end, and "you can't go home" plays far more subtly than in

Star Trek. Maybe it's too subtle, too subdued. We discuss the possibility of furnishing the story with a bigger end-of-the-line payoff. But what? A crash? A death? Who do we kill? Pipe? Too much like *Spinal Tap*, where all the drummers prove spectacularly expendable. John? Maybe. Billy? Might work, but we can't see it yet. Joe? No way, he's the keeper of the flame, he'll carry that weight right into his dotage as bar band frontman. And anyway, what I like about Turner's book is the way the end resists simple conclusions. The band breaks up, the guys move on with their lives, sadder but sort of wiser. It's messy and unresolved, like real life.

Moving on. The whole next day, all the way up into the high country and the Rockies, we talk about strippers. You'd think we were infected by some stripper-watching virus back at the Five. Later in the day the cloud cover lifts and we're treated to big chunks of mountain and sky. This is what we came to see. In the Rockies we pull up at Lake Louise and take pictures of each other on the lake itself, mugging next to a sign that reads Danger: Thin Ice. Then it's out of the Rockies and into the Foothills.

We pull into Calgary at about five p.m. We're going to hook up with my sister Janet for dinner, but she's not off work yet, so we ask a gang of loogans smoking on a street corner where the strip bars are. We get instant, detailed directions to a place called the French Maid.

Well, the French Maid lacks the showbiz slickness and erotic excitement of the Number Five Orange, but that might also be because Rebecca's not here to press herself against anything transparent. As we sit through one stripper after another, we begin to talk about a possible film called *Canadian Stripper*, which would focus on the life of a young woman who slips into exotic dancing at the age of about

——————— lake ontario smells like shit ———————

My motto: never believe everything you read.

seventeen, and would track her career across the country over the course of six years, until she winds up hooking on the streets of Montreal. We discuss how we would resist moralizing and show this young woman even having a sense of humor about the choices she's made and the misfortunes thrown in her path.

Strangely, as we discuss her trials and tragedies, we begin to lose our taste for staring at these dancers. By the time we've talked the idea out, we're more than ready to split. We feel dirty. A pair of filthy, ogling, sexist pigs. Joe Eszterhas and Paul Verhoeven (sans the money). We stagger out into the blowing snow, nauseous with self-contempt. It's that bastard Keith's fault for sucking us into this sleazy shadow world.

We meet my sister for dinner and later check out a club called the Night Gallery. Here we meet a number of Calgary's alterno bon vivants. Janet has seen to it that her actor friends have made it out to meet us, as we're still looking for a Joe and a John. The people here are hilarious, fun, smart. Bruce is a quasi-celebrity, everyone wants to talk to him about his work.

After settling in with the company we've forgotten all about our strip club depression. Then this guy Grant comes running to the table laughing and excited. He takes us down a hallway to show us what's so funny. Next to the club's office is a toilet stall. Not in an enclosed bathroom or anything, it's just right there in the hall. Grant gets down low and points under the stall door. We kneel down for a look. And there we see what has to be the weirdest sight of the entire trip. There's an old guy in there, he's got his cowboy boots off, and he's shaving the corns off his bare feet with a ten-inch hunting blade. Back at the table Bruce sketches the scene into his notebook like it's a storyboard for a film. There's the knife, the feet, the cowboy boots, all as they might appear on screen. He vows to use it somewhere, someday. I don't need to sketch it out. Image like that sticks with you a long time.

Grant tells us a Kurt Cobain story from the time Nirvana played Calgary and stayed at the Westward Hotel. Can't remember it word for word, but it seemed to involve Grant, Kurt, Krist, Dave, possibly Courtney (this is vague), others, drinking and fighting, drugs, a trashed hotel room, livid hotel staffers, bedsheets, an alarm of some kind, threats, broken glass, blood, a shower, possibly the fire department. In Michael Turner's book, the Westward is the hotel Hard Core Logo always stay at when touring through here. So this is where we book in for the night. Good double occupancy rate. Guy at the desk gives us a blank look when we ask for Kurt's room.

One last gasp of pornography before we pack it in. It's three in the morning and we're tanked. We lie in adjacent hotel beds watching a compelling tale of sibling rivalry unfold on the porn channel. Two squabbling sisters, a blonde and a brunette, plot to teach each other a lesson by seducing each other's boyfriends. The blonde has breasts so huge, hard, and round, it looks like she's simply had a pair of bowling balls sewn right into her chest. The brunette is less of a blow-up doll, but there's no question she too has seen the surgeon's knife in hopes of shoring up her thespian credentials. Both seem to be doing a bang-up job of stealing each other's squeezes. As the action heats up, the perfunctory seduction scenes get shorter and shorter until the whole thing degenerates into a series of fast paced intercuts between the sisters humping entire armies of each other's boyfriends. There are so many boyfriends I'm wondering what the hell these gals have to be so possessive and vindictive about. I turn to Bruce to offer a few comments and insights as the credits roll but he's fast asleep. Just as well. Call me a prude, but I have a hard time seeing pornography as a shared experience, especially on, you know, business trips. Two business travelers lying in a double room watching turbofucking on TV. Just seems wrong.

Still, it gets me thinking about bands on tour. I wonder if Joe Dick and Billy Tallent watch the porn channel in their hotel rooms out on the road, and if so, what they might talk about while watching. I have no idea. Makes me realize I don't know them well enough yet. Gotta dig deeper.

A final thought: could this by some fluke be Kurt's old room?

17 January 1995, Toronto

I'm well into dismantling the first draft though a long way from reconstructing a second. Trying to do something about the overlong setup, which begins with John buying a stand-up bass for the band's acoustic reunion benefit show for the

hard core roadshow

Green World Coalition. From here we catch up, one by one, with Joe, who chases a postie for delivering junk mail to his place, Pipe, who learns of the gig from a poster while delivering garbage to the dump, and Billy, who is spacing out at home, playing guitar feedback. There are answering machine messages, trips to the Money Mart to cash welfare cheques, confessions to camera about bad feelings left over from the band's last breakup, Joe blames Billy for his deafness in one ear, etc., etc. Finally they play the benefit show, twenty minutes into what would be the film if we shot today. After this the whole "convincing the band" process begins again when Joe talks the guys into taking the show on tour. Again, the other three guys go through moments of resistance, soul-searching, and confession, before the tour is actually arranged. Then there are all the details related to arranging the tour: getting cassettes and T-shirts to sell, renting a van and so on. All these details interest me; this is stuff you rarely get to see in a film, the normally boring, practical shitwork attended to. All this may well have to go at some point though. Bruce wants to see the band on the road much earlier. Makes sense. Just have to start getting ruthless with this material.

10 February 1995

Wrote a new opening scene. Not a scene, really. A title sequence. It's a Hard Core Logo music video to open the film. I like scripts that start and end with a bang. So I have this idea for the song "Rock 'n' Roll Is Fat and Ugly." There's a weird rock star barbecue where we see malignantly obese versions of Madonna and Elvis and The Stones and Aerosmith and Michael Jackson all chowing down on these bloody shanks of meat, eating like there's no tomorrow, like they can never get enough of it. Then we pan to a big boiling cannibal's pot full of naked teenagers. The word FANS is painted on the pot. We see a kid being turned on a spit over a fire. Record company suits in rodent masks chase around fighting over the scraps and leftovers. The megastars and their minions are eating the flesh of their own fans, of the very people who made them what they are. The guys from Hard Core Logo arrive on the scene like avenging angels to try and save the kids and kick some rock star butt. They do hand to hand combat with the record weasels as the big stars cower, but then Madonna takes charge and swings a big Gatling gun around on them and opens fire, riddling the band through and through. Blood squibs all over the place as the boys are martyred in their tracks. It's rock 'n' roll Pasolini and Peckinpah rolled into one.

Feel pretty confident no one has ever opened a movie like this. Faxed it off to the office. Bruce calls me back and he's laughing so hard he can barely talk. In the background Brian can be heard laughing and the words "lawsuit" and "sick fuck" filter through. Which suggests I'm on the right track. In fact, this scene is a breakthrough. Like throwing down a gauntlet. Now the rest of the picture has to live up to the lofty expectations established here at the git-go.

Beyond this, I've been hacking and slashing at the "context-setting" and "character-development" shots and lines from the first act. This thing's gotta hit the road before the end of the first act, or it ain't a road movie. But I fear losing the lovely elegiac quality to the story (cannibal barbecue opening aside) established in the separate introductions to the four members of Hard Core Logo. Page upon page of great words, many from Turner's book, are being excised in the interest of economy and pace. Such is screenwriting. You kill your own. You eat your young. Or, in the case of adaptations, somebody else's.

21 February 1995

The new draft is finished. Feeling pretty good about it, as I always do with the latest draft of anything. I drop it off at Bruce's office and swagger home to celebrate. This one rocks. Eventually I get a call from Brian. His response is subdued. Script's good, but . . . it's still too dialogue-driven, the tour takes too long to get going, it's still not a movie, it's still too tied to the book, etc., etc., etc. So the honeymoon's over, I guess.

The new draft is nonetheless going in to Telefilm and the OFDC with preliminary budgets, so that we can get on the agenda for the next phase of financing. I've already been paid installments for script development via both agencies. In this next phase the agencies see whether or not they were right to fund the piece in the first place. The new start date for preproduction is May 15th, according to Brian. We'll be hard pressed, especially if I'm a couple of drafts away from making this thing filmable.

22 February 1995

Since Brian has been getting busier with *The Rez* series, we've been working with a new producer, Armand Leo. Great guy, Armand. Smart, fun to work with, loaded with ideas, almost all of them good. Until now. Armand and Bruce call me in for a chat, then ask quite seriously, What if the band were from Toronto and the tour was out to the East Coast?

Then we might as well rip up the script and start from scratch, I say. East is east and West is west, and never the twain shall meet. The eastbound tour suggestion is motivated by interprovincial film bureaucracy and nothing else. Our provincial sponsors, the OFDC, tend to prefer having their scratch spent in Ontario, and Bruce and Armand obviously fear losing it if we shoot the whole film out of province. But a tour beginning in Toronto and ending in Halifax means something entirely different from a tour that inscribes a vast oval of at least two thousand miles out West. It's entirely a question of landscape, geography, and the psychology of wide empty space. Out West the journey is much more epic and quixotic. As I have it in the script: four guys playing five nights over three thousand miles . . . At this level you do it for love.

Then there's politics and history. Hard Core Logo are Vancouver boys, born and bred. Dontchewguys know how radically different that is from being Toronto boys? (They do, they just don't care about it as much as this ex-Vancouver boy does.) My defense mounts into a tirade about how it's gotta be out West, or not at all. Though it later occurs to me that my "distinct region" rhetoric flies in the face of my usual federalist leanings, my passion in the moment wins the day. We move on to discuss the possibility of seeking financing outside the province to preserve the story as it is. Possibly even American money.

27 February 1995

Another meeting at Telefilm. They've got the second draft of the script, and we're here to see if they have any inclination to hand over our production funding. I'm much more relaxed this time as I sit down with Bruce, Brian, Armand, and once again, Michelle and John.

So. Whatcha think? How're ya liking it?

Well, says Michelle. There is clearly something worthwhile in the material, but why are these band guys talking about amps and speakers in Act Three, when they should be talking about, or doing something about, their problems and differences? Why the big focus on trivial details? Why do these guys do all their most important talking to the camera, instead of to one another? Why doesn't this script answer the questions it raises?

Oh Christ. Again I explain that these guys have a lot of issues they've never been able to discuss openly amongst themselves, that it's a realistic portrait of the tensions that exist in small-time bands and of the characters of a bunch of arrested adolescents, that not all questions are meant to be answered, and blah blah blah blah blah to no obvious avail. Anyway, the fight scene at the climax is a great ending, I say.

Sorry, says Michelle, you mean the big fight on stage between Joe and Billy at the end is the "resolution"? They come to blows and part ways leaving a big mess behind? Is that what I call a "resolution"?

Okay, she's got me there. A fight isn't necessarily a resolution. We know that Billy goes off to Seattle to play with a more promising band, and Joe returns to Vancouver and puts out a classified ad for new musicians to start up another band. Is that a resolution? Well it's an ending, anyway. We have thought of killing off John or Billy, but my death scenes have seemed too overwrought, out of step with the rest of the story.

So is it such a big problem ending a film with a big fight and a breakup? It is if it feels like an issue has been evaded.

The question is, has an issue been evaded? I didn't think so, but maybe Michelle's right. She knows she's right, and assures us there's further to go in script development than we think. No production financing until they're satisfied with the script. Fine. Agreed. I'll just keep writing until they break down and give us the money. Bruce is getting impatient, though, and at the end of the meeting he makes my heart stop when he threatens to abandon this project if we aren't greenlighted by June. Michelle doesn't seem to be too rattled by this. I am.

14 March 1995

Solid writing for over two weeks has yielded a third draft. It's a lot like the second draft, but tighter, a bit faster, and the dialogue is way better. I hack out a new set of notes for Telefilm vaguely outlining plans for further improvement. If they sound a bit preachy, it's because I'm still feeling a bit defensive after the last big meeting and I figure the best defense is a good offense.

```
NOTES ON 3RD DRAFT, 14 MARCH 1995

The THIRD DRAFT of HARD CORE LOGO
(13 March 1995) sees a number of changes
and improvements. Draft by draft, the means
of telling this story become more cinematic
and less literary. The narrative throughline
tracking the development — and degeneration —
of Joe and Billy's relationship is stronger
than ever. There are now musical performances
included which will allow viewers to see for
themselves what a great band HCL are/were.
```

—————— hard core roadshow ——————

The band's interaction with fans is now
also beefed up considerably, to show more
clearly how they are/were regarded by "the
people." There is a slightly reduced reliance
on such devices as voice-overs and interviews,
and where possible, the narrative is advanced
in expanded scenes. We're now looking at
something that's leaner, meaner, less talky
yet more involving than previous drafts.
It should otherwise be noted that we are
still largely propelling story and revealing
character by fairly unconventional means.

HARD CORE LOGO is a cinematic document; it
is not a documentary, though it makes use of
documentary devices. It happens to take place
in a world where four vivid characters play
phone tag, get interviewed, tell stories and
lies, think out loud, make candid confessions
to the audience that they would never make to
each other, stab each other in the back, avoid
painful reckonings, and communicate best mainly
when they are performing on stage. We have used
the term "collage" to describe the process of
telling this story. There are FOUR points of
view. JOE, BILLY, JOHN, and PIPE have wildly
different agendas and reasons for going on the
tour in the story. Until the final act, they
rarely discuss their differences openly. This
story's evasions are in many ways its most
honest and intelligent feature. The tensions
build and simmer beneath the surface of most

lake ontario smells like shit

scenes in which the four of them are together, until the final act.

The entire road trip is a journey towards a reckoning with an unresolved past and this reckoning has a huge impact on everyone's future. The farther the band travels, the harder it is to keep the past at bay. When all the tensions finally erupt into violence during a show in Edmonton, Joe and Billy are finally released from their tortured partnership, and from the bonds of the past. Are they changed as a result of their journey? Not in any larger- than-life sense that would satisfy the story editors at Disney; but they are changed in the sense that they are able, in their early thirties, to turn away from something that had consumed their youth, and get on with their lives as adults. For Billy and Joe (who have "never played music without each other") this means taking new directions in rock 'n' roll. For John it means smashing his bass and getting on with his career; and for Pipe it likewise means putting away the drums and getting on with a blue-collar existence.

This is a movie about four punks lurching into adulthood after a prolonged adolescence. The questions "What's next for you guys?" and "What are you going to do after this tour?" dog the band throughout the story. What these questions mean, in a broader sense, is "What are you going to do with your life?" Like many people nowadays, these guys are having too much trouble grappling with the past to be able to answer questions about the future with any certainty. The questions themselves are <u>the</u> questions for many people out there in their twenties and early thirties. We expect that our intended audience will understand and relate to this material without expecting the characters to undergo mythical movie-land transformations by the end of their journey. Punk scorns the very idea of such wish-fulfillment fantasies as cynical corporate soma for fools. For punks a journey ending in eye-opening disillusionment is better than one ending in manufactured triumph.

Does HARD CORE LOGO answer the questions it raises? Absolutely . . . in a backhanded way. Answers are realistic, grim, and bittersweet; and yet there is hope, especially for Joe, who reaches the end of his road of trials, then plugs ahead, doing the only thing he can do that validates his existence.

What further changes and improvements can be made before the script goes before the camera? The role of JOHN will be clarified further. He is our sentimental narrator, the voice that brings a sense of order and poetry to the alternately grim and funny journey. What motivates him to keep a journal? Does he hope to sell his story and profit by it in some cynical way? Or is he merely bearing witness to the demise of Hard Core Logo? Up until now, we've suggested that John is trying to do both: to both eulogize the journey and to exploit it. As we continue to polish the script, we hope to show in clear and simple ways that this is exactly what John is doing. He is the man with "one foot in and one foot out" and he tries to keep his balance to the very end. One very punk possibility for John is to show him burning his diary at the end of the story — a way of showing that the events of the story are too important and personal for him to profit from them.

As for JOE and BILLY, we will continue to polish, hone, and clarify the arc of their relationship, to look for connections and details to push . . . whatever it takes to clarify and strengthen the story as it pertains to them.

28 March 1995

There's talk of showing the script to MTV. Turns out Allen Gregg (the Conservative pollster guy turned entertainment biz guy) at Viacom Canada has been hyping Bruce in general and *Hard Core Logo* in particular to the development honcho at MTV (which is a Viacom subsidiary). At least the script is getting a positive response in the commercial world. MTV is getting into film production and distribution. In some ways *Hard Core* is an ideal film for them. Be nice for the film to be picked up in advance by a large U.S. distributor; we might be able to bypass a lot of the government money we're having trouble getting, and unlike most Canadian films, *HCL* might then be seen by more than a couple thousand people.

On the other hand, there's the chance that "minor changes" will be demanded (most film deals being, to some degree, deals with the devil).

Could we maybe turn Vancouver into, say, Seattle? Or better still, L.A.?

Could we maybe make the band sort of a formerly huge metal band, instead of local punk heroes?

Could we, for God's sake, cut all references to Saskatchewan?

Could we maybe make it sexier? Dumb it down a little? Turn the band members into superheroes, each with a special power of his own?

Could we fix it so the lead singer's girlfriend has to be rescued from evil bikers? Hey great script! Who can we get to rewrite it? How about the wit responsible for *Airheads*?

Could we maybe get rid of this Bruce McDonald and bring in our own guy? Maybe the guy who directed *Airheads*? Or the guy who directed *The Crow*?

And the cast: Callum Rennie, Bernie Coulson ... it's a joke, right? Who can we really get to launch this picture? Depp? Keannu? Steven Dorff? When's Luke Perry's hiatus from *90210*? How about Poison for the music?

29 March 1995

Shadow Shows last night with Bruce, Brian, Armand, Jeff Rogers (who manages Crash Test Dummies and Rusty), and

Meryn Caddell. Meryn reads through a monologue that she and Jeff hope Bruce will transform into a film along the lines of Spalding Gray's *Swimming to Cambodia*. The monologue is entertaining and seductive, very well written and well read, taking the listener on a tour of the sidestreets of Meryn's life, past and present.

Later we go for dinner and drinks. Later still I'm left with Meryn and Jeff talking drunkenly about the paths each of us took to get "where we are today." Meryn and Jeff have seen considerable success in their respective fields and speak of knowing from childhood what their adult careers would be. I had no such early convictions about myself. Meryn, being a friend of Michael Turner's and knowing next to nothing about me, demands to know exactly what "qualifies" me to write the screenplay to *Hard Core Logo*. Good question. I do not perform my work publicly as poets tend to do these days. I have not grown up in public, artistically. It's difficult to explain to people that though one's body of work is so far unknown, it might still "qualify" one for such jobs as screenplay adaptations of books by up-and-coming Canadian poets. Instead of finding the words to say this, I offer the scotch-fueled boast that I qualify because I am simply one of the best screenwriters in the country, period. Bit of a silence follows this. Then I realize it's time to go.

Weaving home on my bicycle, I keep checking my shoulder, wondering how that big ugly chip got there. Guess I'm touchier than I thought about my unheraldedness. By the time I put my bike away and fumble for my keys, the boast has replayed a thousand times in my head. The shame is acute. Here in Canada such boasts are poor form; they make you sound so American.

hard core roadshow

4 April 1995

Bruce went down to New York with Armand over the weekend and lost his fucking mind. Trip was supposed to be all business: he was going to meet the guys from MTV who were supposedly interested in kicking some money into *HCL*. I don't think he made it to that meeting.

Bruce with pal Joey.

What he did do, though, was hang out with Joey Ramone, who introduced him to Debbie Harry and other old guard punk/new wave types. Don't know exactly what else happened, except when Bruce and Armand got back, I was told that Bruce is off the project as director and Mina (*Double Happiness*) Shum was being approached to direct.

I ask for some clarification: What. The. Fuck. Are. You. Talking. About?

He can't exactly explain.

Hang up. Mind starts racing. So what's going wrong? What's with Bruce anyway? Is he bored? Why? Is he unhappy about the script? Did someone with money nibble at *Yummy Fur*? God knows what'll happen if Mina comes on board this project. Probably means good-bye Noel as she rolls up her sleeves and "puts her stamp" on the script and makes a radically different animal of this project. I am not happy.

Apparently we're going to Cleveland to meet her on the weekend.

Cleveland. What the fuck.

Guess she's doing publicity for her film or something. I hear *Double Happiness* is a very fine film, an assured feature directing début, so full marks to Mina. I just know that without Bruce, there's hardly any point to *Hard Core* at all. Whole thing's about two steps from going over a cliff. I'm drinking myself into a stupor as I write this.

8 April 1995

Seems a deal could not be reached to procure Mina's services. Seems her agent is demanding about a third of our total budget for her directing fee, now she's so hot. More important though, after taking the trouble to scare the bejesus out of me, Bruce was kind enough to sit down and read my newest draft, the draft I was finishing while he was in New York. In a nutshell, he loves it, and he's all fired up to move ahead again as director.

A small flutter of indecision for him; a hurricane rocking my world. When the power lies with others to change a project you love, knock you off it, or kill it outright, you can't help but feel naked and vulnerable. Bruce makes one point clear: he wants the movie to be tougher and harder-edged than anything he's done to date.

12 April 1995

Bruce calls to say he's now thinking of turning Hard Core Logo, the band, into women, into an all-girl band.
  ... Noel? Ya there?
  ... Yeah Bruce.
  Don't panic, man, he says, just kick it around, sleep on it, see whatcha think, get back to me tomorrow ... 'Cause I'm pretty sure it's the direction we're moving in.
  And that's that. Sit there totally numb, ponder the possibility that a parasite has begun feasting on Bruce's frontal lobe. There's no question now, this project is floundering. The director's vision is all over the place. The director obviously has no fucking idea what kind of movie he wants to make, or why he even wants to make it. Guy's begging for a quick fix. Someone probably told him the script needs to be more ... I don't know, more something ... more shocking, more flashy, more unexpected, and more PC all at the same time.
  So sure, turn Hard Core into a girl band. That'll solve everything. Great idea. The political contortionists at the agencies will love it. They'll hail it as a step in the right direction. They never did seem too comfortable with our story about four raunchy losers on the road, their ugly opinions zinging around a cramped, stinking van. Four punks in a van? Gosh, what if they say hurtful, disrespectful, sexist things? What if all they do is trash each other or our cherished institutions? Jeepers, what if they're not very nice? Movie like this might give the wrong impression about Canadians and what they stand for.

I follow Siobhan around the house, throwing my hands up, asking rhetorical questions in scornful tones: Does Bruce think our entire audience consists of politically correct bureaucrats? Doesn't he know the hell he's putting me through, changing his mind like this? Who the hell does he think he is, anyway? Siobhan is more or less sympathetic on cue. Finally I ask the question this has all been leading to: Okay, what if I turn HCL into a female band?

Siobhan stops, looks at me. I don't think so, she says.

You know, one of those pussy power foxcore chick rock groups? L7 meets The Runaways? No?

Siobhan says no. Different story. She's right. If the four women in the band are in their mid-thirties like the HCL guys, they probably won't be as endearingly blind to their own foibles as Joe, Billy, John, and Pipe are. You can't substitute women for men and hope the story still works on "male" terms.

I spend the evening poring over the script, resolved to call Bruce in the morning, armed with reasons to continue down the path we're already on. But I end up looking at the script through the eyes of an imaginary, hypercritical Bruce. I see nothing but holes and weaknesses, nothing but good reasons to call for drastic changes. It's a long night of nagging doubts, micro and macro, about this project, about my entire life. Thoughts about the "endearing blindness" of my characters segue easily into a frank internal dialogue concerning my own delusion that I will ever come close to doing good, let alone great, work. That my best years are still ahead of me.

13 April 1995

Forced cheerfulness as I call Bruce, explain that while the idea of a film about a girl band is interesting in itself and would be the basis of a very cool rock 'n' roll picture, it simply doesn't fit the idea we are well into developing. One can't simply transpose sex without changing the foundations of the story altogether. Would a female Hard Core Logo reunite in the same way, in their thirties, for the same reasons as our current characters? Doubt it. None of the women artists or musicians I've ever met are dumb, desperate, or immature enough to put themselves through what these guys put themselves through to try and capture a little lost glory. Whereas with the male musicians this story is typical, if not archetypal. With such a fundamental change in character you have to be writing an entirely different story.

And that's all I have to say about that, Bruce-man. Except also, if we go that route, I'm going to have to cut you into wee pieces and feed you to seagulls.

Okay, just checkin', Bruce says. Makin' sure no tern's left unstoned. Carry on, man.

22 April 1995

The search for an actor to play Joe Dick has gone about as well as the search for the Oklahoma City bomber. We've considered all kinds of people, but no one seems "real" enough. Bruce has been talking about casting his pal Hugh Dillon, the lead singer from the band Headstones.

Not sure what I think about this. Saw Hugh play the tough guy/villain in Bruce's last picture, styled like a spike-haired leather-clad maniac out of *Mad Max*. You just don't find guys like that in northern Canadian towns, where *Dance Me Outside* is set. Hugh's acting was fine within the parameters of his small role, but Bruce is talking about having this guy carry *Hard Core Logo*. Not a safe bet by any standard. This worries

———————— lake ontario smells like shit ————————

Real enough:
Hugh Dillon.

me and I urge Bruce to keep looking. He gives me one of those polite but utterly noncommittal "I'll take it under advisement" answers that I've fallen into the habit of giving at script meetings.

6 *May 1995*

To a warehouse where the band Swamp Baby rehearse. Here Bruce and I meet the guys who are making the music that will be the classic punk sound of Hard Core Logo. Peter Moore (our music producer/composer on the project) has just finished recording an indie CD with these guys and he claims they've got the chops for this job. Plus they come real cheap. The band's space is full of ragged throwaway furniture, empties, equipment cases, with posters and carpet tacked to walls. In such hellholes the world over monster rock tunes are written.

Swamp Baby's members are mainly guys in their thirties who came up through the Toronto punk scene. Now they play largely throwback 70s-inspired hard rock, like Soundgarden et al. But tonight, for an audience of two, they play one-two-three-fah! punk rock. (We've decided to ditch the book's "acoustic reunion" idea and go electric. It'll play better on film.) They run through eight songs, most of which sound like plausible early 80s punk and two or three of them absolutely kick. Peter tells us that they wrote all the songs and recorded the first demos in something like ten days. Which is amazing when you consider that they all have day jobs.

Afterwards Steve Cowell, Swamp Baby's singer, speaks highly of his pal Hugh Dillon, lead singer for Headstones. Steve sounds just a little wistful when he talks about how Hugh's gonna take these songs and make 'em his own. Plus he's gonna do a bang-up job as the lead in the movie. Gong! This catches me off guard. Hugh Dillon is Bruce's confirmed choice to play Joe Dick? Others know about it? It's a sure thing? Yes. Swamp Baby will record these songs, then Hugh will come in and dub his own vocals over the tracks, replacing Steve's reedy yowl. And then he will star in the movie.

*

Questions about bands like Swamp Baby: what is it like being a footsoldier in the rock 'n' roll trenches for nearly twenty years? What is it like to plug away at a music career while making the bulk of your income at some "day job"? What hopes and dreams of glory are left to you in this business as you turn the corner towards forty? Do you still really think you're going to get signed to a major label, have a hit record, headline large clubs or theaters? Are there any illusions left at all? Or are you in it for love, for the moment when you hit the stage, for the rush of playing for a crowd, however small? Many are, pure and simple. Yet there must be hundreds of bands out there with guys in their thirties, not-yet-successful bands, never-was bands, who believe they have a chance of breaking out, making records, touring, making a living. Must remember to address the age question in the script.

12 May 1995

Bruce saw Callum Rennie out in Vancouver a few days ago, gave him my number. So Callum calls. He's in town guesting on a TV series. He's having a busy year, playing one of the leads in John L'Ecuyer's film *Curtis's Charm*, and doing plenty of guest spots on TV series, playing varieties of cool or angry guy. He suggests we meet up.

I find him on the crowded patio of The Black Bull on Queen, in jeans an intentional size too big, battered brown boots, a bowling shirt, reddish dink cap, shades. American cigs. Redneck chic. He's one of the lean ones with a studied sense of cool. Every inch an actor. I go to order us beer, but he asks for coffee. He explains that he got a lifetime's worth of serious drinking out of the way during his twenties, and now, in his thirties, he doesn't want drinking to get in the way of some serious acting.

Exploratory conversation: we talk about people we know in common out in Vancouver, about likes and dislikes, about the film. Callum is candid about many things, more or less tells me up front that he is often considered "difficult" by TV people. He hates to be given stupid lines, phrases that people don't use in real life. Callum is grooming himself for the bigtime, for stardom, though he's too cool to broadcast this openly. You can see it in his role choices, though: hipsters, loners, outsiders, rebels, charmers. He doesn't look like someone who would take a goofy or unsympathetic character role, because like most people who want to be stars, he understands the connection between the role and the actor's own persona. If he is difficult about dialogue it is because he doesn't want to appear foolish. And he's right. Any good-enough-looking screen actor who wants to go all the way should take this kind of care from the beginning. I like this guy, the way I always like people who know what they're doing and where they're going. Look forward to working with him on the film.

16 May 1995

Just completed yet another draft (unless otherwise specified, I'm always writing a new draft of this fucking thing), and it bears only passing resemblance to the ones cited above. I'm hoping this is the one that puts us into the production money. Bruce likes it: it's tougher, cooler, more emotional, more raw, more rock 'n' roll in every way, than previous drafts.

Each time I take a pass through the script, I view the new work as the definitive one, and I want all other inferior copies destroyed. The earlier drafts are products of a stubborn fidelity to the source book. These days I'm thinking less and less about Michael Turner's literary intentions and more about my own intention to write the best rock 'n' roll movie ever made. Moving slowly into uncharted territory. With each new draft I feel like this becomes more "my" document, "my" story. Screenwriters should beware such pride. After all, the picture will come out and the only thing people will care about is that it is "A Bruce McDonald Movie," starring Callum and Hugh. I am but a middle man between book and screen, a mere translator. That's the way it is in film. The screenplay is invisible, and so, for the most part, is the screenwriter.

*

Business news gleaned from eavesdropping on Brian's occult phone chats with mysterious financial overlords: we need a commitment from a Canadian distributor before the agencies will finance production. Haven't got one yet. Cineplex, Alliance, and others haven't rushed to snap this one up. Maybe I really am blind to the script's flaws because I find it hard to believe there aren't any takers for this thing. Meanwhile the CBC is nibbling. Call me crazy, but I just don't see *HCL* as a movie-of-the-week.

Armand Leo has quit to be the production manager on the Kids in the Hall feature for Paramount. Seems he couldn't afford to stick around through a long development period, as there just wasn't enough money coming in. I've heard that a friend of his in Vancouver named Christine Somethingor-other is going to pick up the pieces and co-produce with Brian. Makes sense, since we'll be shooting out there. None of this is my department, but somewhere down the line it will come home to roost right on top of this work I've been doing alone in my room all these months.

25 May 1995

Bruce lives in Kensington Market, on the top floor of a converted office building. This is where our first real production powwow takes place. A warm evening. I arrive and meet our Director of Photography, Miroslav Baszak, who shot

Dance Me Outside, *Highway 61*, and *Roadkill*. Also here is Michael Pacek, who edited these films. Guys who go way back with Bruce.

Last to arrive are Brian and the new Vancouver-based producer we've inherited via Armand, Christine Haebler. This is the woman who is going to plug us into the city we're making the film in, the woman who is going to make a lot of hard decisions and thousands of phone calls. I've heard she's never actually produced a feature before (there have been shorts, and she has experience in various other areas of feature production). So I'm curious, what's she like? First impression: she seems tall. Even though she isn't, especially. The impression of height derives from diva attitude, good posture, a sort of confidence. (Already I'm thinking of her as "La Haebler.") A notch or two north of thirty. When I hear her bold laugh for the first time I am struck by a second impression: the broad's gonna kick some butt on this picture. Turns out she's been aware of the film since the first draft of the script.

So here we all are: the braintrust. And for the first time I am pulled into discussions that involve other areas of expertise. A whole new layer of input at last. We talk about film stock and decide that shooting super 16mm is preferable to 35 mm, because we'll get a better rough-and-ready look, more like a documentary than a slick feature. Miro can do a lot more handheld work with the smaller camera, and this will allow the crew to get through their setups faster and further exploit the verité style.

We discuss a four week shooting schedule. It'll be tight, but again, if we can turn our limitations into strengths, we'll be able to shoot a few more script pages a day than larger productions.

All of these issues lead to a discussion of my domain: the style and cinematic language established in the screenplay. As of tonight what we have is a script that is a straight drama with breaks where Joe, Billy, John, and Pipe stop and talk to the camera, candidly disclosing their hopes and fears, beefs and disappointments. In these moments, the action basically stops, the fourth wall is knocked down. It uses documentary devices without having the film pretend to be a documentary. The problem with this style, Michael Pacek astutely observes, is that it tends to get coy and cloying, and it's being done in too many other films now. All these knowing confessions cluttering up the narrative throughline. Miro agrees. So does Christine.

All this time I've been working on content. I've thought a lot about the film's style. So has Bruce. But now I realize that we have to be a lot more specific about the film's narrative frame. We agree that the moments of confession to camera are important, because the four leads are guys who have trouble being honest with each other and instead use the camera as primary confidante. What do we have now? Something that seems to have fallen through the conceptual cracks between documentary and drama.

While the script has been reading well from draft to draft, and has had compliments on its dialogue, scene structure, and other components, it isn't in fact working for either the cameraman or the film editor, the two people who will be closest to the process during production and post-production. It's clear that the script I've written can't be the script we're going to shoot, not if the basic cinematic conceit isn't nailed down. If we're not careful we could end up with something completely laughable.

When the others leave, Bruce and I look at the problem

from a variety of angles, but get nowhere. We agree to come to agreement ASAP on what the hell kind of picture this is going to be.

2 June 1995

I've resolved to rent as many videos as it takes to find elements of style that I can steal for *HCL*. I bring home a big stack. Watch *A Hard Day's Night* for the twentieth time. The amateurish Clash film, *Rude Boy*. Nicholas Roeg's *Performance* for the third time. Nothing much I can use here.

Then a breakthrough with Antonioni's *Blow-Up*. I'm almost embarrassed to admit it, but I've never seen it until now. An amazing film, supercool (i.e., ironic enough to remain hip today), shot with a keen eye for the hypocrisies of the "liberated" 60s. I'd read that the film was a murder mystery about a photographer who accidentally snaps a picture containing evidence of a murder. I find that it is in fact a character portrait of a young egomaniac in Swinging London who discovers that the world actually doesn't revolve around him. There's barely any plot to speak of.

This is a loose and ponderous film that in examining the character of David Hemmings' photographer, examines the character of the era with a thoroughly jaundiced, voyeuristic eye. The photographer's lens is both a key to the weird reality around him, and a buffer against it. Swinging London becomes a combination of photographer's set and specimen jar. Unlike so many now desperately uncool "cool" films of the era, *Blow-Up* stands the test of time by bearing witness to the moment, rather than, fatally, celebrating it. The photographer's camera is itself a cold but crucial character in the film. I'm thinking about the camera's role in *HCL*, but haven't quite figured out how far to take the characters' acknowledgment of its presence. For example, are there some scenes where the fourth wall is up, and some where it is down? Should it be down in all scenes? Still have to decide what the narrative rules are going to be.

One more thing about *Blow-Up*. One of the best scenes has Hemmings passing through a Yardbirds gig and ending up with the splintered neck of Jeff Beck's smashed guitar in his hands out on the street. A highly prized souvenir which he then tosses aside on a whim. A very quotable image about the disposability of pop, and one which could well find its way into the script.

I also watch a documentary on the history of punk which superficially traces punk's origins and trickle-down manifestations in Britain and America. What takes me by surprise is how nostalgic I feel for the period on seeing the hair, the jackets, the leather and studs, the sneers, and above all the smooth-faced young members of the Pistols, the Clash, the Ramones, the Damned, and so on, playing to pogoing crowds. While there are remnants of a twenty-year-old punk style everywhere you look these days, the vintage item captured on aging celluloid seems almost quaint now. The then-new sense of ironic coolness established by punk now looks, in retrospect, like a kooky fad, a costume party in some alternative Beach Blanket Bingo where the krazy kids are just out to have fun shocking the old folks. Surely it was more than this! But the images have a reductive quality that the film's context-setting narration can't compensate for. I am left feeling that punk, the great kicker of sacred cows, is now itself the subject of flabby nostalgia, a quirky museum exhibit, an aberration in the development of mainstream rock, a mainstream that now generously forgives and embraces punk like it's the errant sibling who crawled home to die after a few years of misguided rebellion and dangerous experimentation.

The critics have always taken punk's stylized alienation more seriously than "the industry" has. Punk is an established field of historical inquiry for rock musicologists, who tend to theorize it as a mix of sophisticated Dada-esque art-school irony and brute working-class rage, with spit as the ultimate emblem of contempt for art, authority, performer, and self. The credit for inventing punk has been assigned, reassigned, and disputed in near-scholarly articles for years. The punk years are a robust historical period, especially with the twentieth anniversary creeping up. The writers are writing and the bands are reuniting. In Vancouver the Subhumans are back at it. Saw the reunited Buzzcocks at Lee's Palace a while back. There are rumblings about a Clash reunion. Wouldn't be surprised to hear of a Sex Pistols reunion at some point. Or someone opening a punk show lounge in Vegas.

3 June 1995

David Griffith and I have been corresponding via e-mail about our *Gotterdammerung* script. Dave has launched into a new draft of it, and I've been keeping up my end, sending off notes and new scene suggestions. The story is about a rock band who are duped into signing a "management" contract with the devil, only to find themselves transformed into messengers of doom and possessors of youthful souls, sort of the Four Bikers of the Apocalypse. In the course of refining our story, I come up with this list of band archetypes.

LEAD SINGER/FRONTMAN: The demagogue with the message, more interested in his role as messenger than in the music itself.

LEAD GUITARIST: The real musician who cares more for riffs, licks, and chord progressions than for the lead singer's messianic message. The lead singer's best buddy and songwriting partner since childhood. The friendship hits the rocks only after the band is successful, when the guys start believing the hype and thinking they can do even better on their own. (Think Jagger-Richards, Lennon-McCartney, Strummer-Jones, the guys in *Spinal Tap* . . . the archetype plays out over and over.)

BASS PLAYER: The quiet one who shuns the spotlight and enjoys his wealth in aristocratic seclusion (usually the art collector, horse owner, or vine grower). A rationalist, he is often called upon to play "conciliator" in the knockdown rows between the singer and lead guitarist.

DRUMMER: Dumb, raving, lunatic party animal. A totally insane force of nature who marches to his own beat and trashes hotel rooms on tour not because he wants to but because he thinks he has to. Usually self-destructive and fucked up. Often marked for death.

Only later do I realize that, but for the bass player's wealth and the doomed drummer, I am really thinking of the guys in *Hard Core Logo*.

4 June 1995

Some graffiti from above the urinal at the Midtown on College that might find a home in the ever cruder, ever tougher *Hard Core Logo*: "I am twelve inches long and five inches around. Interested?" Underneath some wit has written, "Fascinated, but how big is yer cock?" Planning to stick this on the wall of the band's dressing room in Regina.

Return home to a message from Bruce. Wants to know if I'd mind having a story editor to help solve some script problems.

Do I "mind"? What happens if I say yes, I do mind.

Figure I might as well find out, so I call him up and say yes, I do mind. "Story editor" sounds an awful lot like "script doctor." Can't say I'm totally comfortable with the idea. Yet somehow, after a few minutes on the phone with Bruce, I find myself agreeing to meet with a story editor in the next couple of weeks.

All this time I've taken Bruce's silences about the script for tacit approvals. If I've held back these last months from charging alone into more extreme dramatic directions, it's because I haven't felt like I've had the authority to do it, between my responsibility to the book and the director I am "working for."

17 June 1995

Meeting yesterday in the War Room. Present and accounted for are Bruce, Brian, Christine Haebler, John Frizzell, and me. Frizzell is a screenwriter/ story editor/ script doctor, a man about town in the Toronto film scene (also a co-writer on *Dance Me Outside*). Bruce has asked him to story edit *HCL* mainly because he's very good at what he does, but perhaps partly because one of his closest friends is a major force at Telefilm. A good political choice, Frizzell. He can go off on Friday night for drinks with his Telefilm friend and explain how via his bold intervention *Hard Core Logo* has been radically improved, rescued from mediocrity, in fact saved. So, in this defensive state of mind, run my thoughts.

We get down to work and John Frizzell turns out, in fact, to be a thoroughly likable and charming guy. For a vivisectionist. We spend six hours poring over the script and Frizzell genially describes the extent of the malignant cancers running through the entire structure, through every scene, cancers that require immediate radical surgery. This thing will never get close to production funding from Telefilm in the shape it's in, he assures us. He enumerates the problems as I smile and nod, doing what I can to conceal my mounting hostility: the guys in the band are unsympathetic assholes (yeah, so?), the emotional and material stakes are too low (whaddya want, these guys are welfare cases), Bucky Haight is a bore (fine, if your idea of fun is Ru Paul), John Oxenberger's a dull prig (well . . . true), the dialogue is too "on point" and not documentary-like enough (bullshit, the dialogue rocks), there's no story to speak of, the source material is weak, there is no female representation in the script, in fact the whole thing, while having "potential," sucks in its present form. Get the patient to the O.R. and sharpen the scalpels: we're going in.

At the end of the meeting I'm exhausted. I numbly thank Frizzell for his input, all the while wondering how I got saddled with the Dr. Mengele of script doctors. Seeing past my own defensiveness, I have to admit the man is right about a lot of it, maybe even most of it. I don't know. This kind of session leaves your confidence gasping on the ropes. Anyway, Bruce and Christine tell me I've got something like ten days to revive this terminal patient if we're still going to get it past the Telefilm gatekeepers and into production before fall. We all go for drinks to the patio of the Aztec and I sit there traumatized. All I remember from here is Christine patting my hand sympathetically and Bruce kneading my shoulders and giving me a Knute Rockne pep talk.

3.

LET'S GO DOWN TO HOLLYWOOD
(AND SHOOT SOME PEOPLE)

21 June 1995

The horse Clover in *Animal Farm* has a motto: I will work harder! This has become my own motto as I hustle to please my exploiters. I'm a coffee achiever, speeding to meet my deadline. Under this pressure I do my best, most twisted, sickest writing.

Bruce drops by in the mornings for broadstrokes script chats, then I work from noon until three or four in the morning, taking breaks to walk Scout or simply wander through the house like a hollow-eyed ghost, head filled with the vicious, desperate, sad, funny passions and beefs of four over-the-hill punks. Siobhan gives me a wide berth.

Tough love approach to the writing: I'm slapping the script into shape, wiping the smirk off its face, beating the insolent literariness out of it, chiselling away the surface cuteness, pounding out the indie-film quirkiness, cauterizing whatever's left. I look at my entry from 16 May, see that even that "tougher, raunchier" draft was downright cuddly and naive compared to the new streetwise ugly/funny direction. I'm now past the proverbial point where the adapting screenwriter chucks the source material to focus on "the movie that has to be made." Always hated this pompous phrase, advertising as it does the self-importance of movie people. Yet here I am using it and meaning it.

The ch-ch-ch-changes:

Ditched the Green World Coalition business. Plays well in the book, but it's too soft and visually obvious for the film, these punks chafing against hippies. In its place is an edgier, altogether more punk event: an anti-gun rally called Rock Against Guns (songs about guns riddle the discographies of punk icons like the Clash, the Pistols, and most infamously, Nirvana). The story opens with the band reuniting to play a benefit concert for a lobby group called No More Guns, and part of the benefit money is to go to Bucky Haight. Why Bucky? To bring him more centrally into the story, and to introduce the idea of him right at the start.

As Frizzell put it after reading the last draft, the band drops in on some burned-out rocker in the middle of nowhere, so fucking what? Are they changed by Bucky? Only to the extent that he gets them drunk and depresses them with his bittersweet tales about the business that chewed him up and spat him out. His narrative purpose was too vague. Took care of the problem by creating a new story for Bucky, in which his leg has been shot off by an errant hunter on the Prairies, leaving him an embittered cripple. He becomes Joe Dick's personal charity case. Haven't decided yet whether the band's visit to Bucky is for the purpose of delivering the benefit money to him personally. Still working it out.

Following another cool suggestion of Frizzell's, I've changed John (Frizzell simply hates this character) from the know-it-all bookish arty one, into a schizophrenic who loses his lithium prescription during the tour. Which instantly transforms him into a ticking bomb and introduces a tragic and truly unpredictable aspect to all his scenes. I'd been using John's diary entries from the book as voice-overs in the film. Problem is, they made John sound superior and judgmental, the dull prig Frizzell had complained about. I've rewritten these into off-center spacey doggerel that pushes themes of love and betrayal much harder.

Then there's the most important improvement of all: finally

came to terms with the issue of the narrative frame for this movie. It is now *about* a documentary film about the band's reunion tour across Western Canada. There's a director character named Bruce (played by you-know-who) who travels with the band, filming their reunion tour. The real Bruce especially likes this bit; it puts him in the movie, right where he was in his best film, *Roadkill*. Here he can play fun self-reflexive games and continue to add to his own myth-in-progress as a rock 'n' roll director. For months I've resisted this approach because this is precisely the concept for *This Is Spinal Tap*, the ne plus ultra of mockumentaries. None of us wants this film to be compared to *Spinal Tap*. But the concept works for us; it brings the movie alive and literally makes the camera a character. Bruce and the camera fight with the guys. The guys fight back, staring out at what will be the film's audience, telling it to fuck off and die, thereby attacking the medium itself in very punk terms.

23 June 1995

Writing nonstop, one eye on the calendar. Must . . . get . . . script . . . to . . . Telefilm . . . by . . . end . . . of . . . month. Small problem: Siobhan and I are also moving (again!) to a new apartment at the end of the month. No time for packing. I can feel the pressure, literally feel the producers waiting for me to finish.

In the evening Bruce calls, asks if I need a break. (Yes!) Wants me to come see Billy Cowsill play at the Horseshoe. Billy Cowsill is an old-time rocker on the Vancouver scene. Christine had suggested him as a possible Bucky Haight. Though we're satisfied with Julian Richings for the role, Bruce wants to check out any diamonds-in-the-rough that may be lurking out there. Billy dropped by the office earlier today and Bruce spent several hours with him, just talking, listening to Billy's rock 'n' roll stories. Bruce tells me all about Billy's trip to the bottom and the miracle of how he lived to talk about it. "Guy's the enchilada, man."

To the Horseshoe. Billy takes the stage to thunderous cheering from a fairly crowded house. He is beanpole skinny, fifty years old, with wispy black hair, a weathered blade of a face, but the long-lashed eyes of a boy. He's dressed in pointy cowboy boots and head-to-toe black denim. He proves to be a solid, earnest frontman and his band, the Blue Shadows, sound like a cross between the Beatles and the Everly Brothers. The songs are pure ear candy, jammed with hummable hooks and flawless vocal harmonies. Billy cut his popster teeth in the Cowsills back in the 60s, a family band that Bernard Slade apparently used as the model for *The Partridge Family*. Though we don't hold this against him.

As the crowd dances and Billy stands strumming at his mike, toothpick legs spread wide, grinning when not singing, I ponder his viability as a drugged-out underground rock legend in *Hard Core Logo*. The pros: Billy had some harrowing and tragic years living on the street, drinking, drugging, hopelessly lost. The wear and tear shows on him, no question, which is a plus for our purposes. The cons: weathered he may be, but not in a way that says "junkie," and certainly not in a way that screams "punk." When I think of Bucky I think Iggy or Nick Cave or Johnny Thunders, not Billy Cowsill.

We meet Billy backstage afterwards. I ask him if he feels like he has a connection to Bucky Haight, and he talks candidly about being a burned-out rocker. We are interrupted by a fan. A musician actually, who gushes about seeing Billy play years ago, a pivotal moment that inspired him to do the same thing with his own life. He speaks of the debt he owes to Billy, and slips him a demo tape. I think of Joe Dick approaching his idol Bucky Haight for the first time, but there's something different here: these people are country popsters, not punks. The guy moves off as soon as Billy graciously thanks him and wishes him all the best. Then Billy leans over and says, "Ya gotta encourage the young pups. They're the lifeblood, man." A last glance at the "young pup" as he leaves the room. Guy's got to be at least thirty-seven.

After we leave Bruce tells me he's now, after all, truly confirmed in his choice of Julian Richings for Bucky.

25 June 1995

Head's fulla rock thoughts. I stick them in Joe's and John's mouths for the new opening scene to the movie. The camera intercuts between them.

                JOE

Logo's a Greek word, okay? Means symbol or sign. The hard core punk logo is this circle with an A inside it. Means Direct Action. Means anarchy. Means "Question Authority." That's what punk was all about. You question the world around you. You don't like the answers you're getting, it's like, "fuck you." That's what we were all about: FUCK YOU!

                JOHN

Mainstream rock is ten percent inspiration, ninety percent corporation. That's a one hundred percent guaranteed true cliché.

> JOE
>
> Take the fuckin Rolling Stones. Do we really need to watch these millionaires stand over a dead horse and hosepipe it into the sidewalk? The horse is dead. Leave it alone.
>
> JOHN
>
> We were all inspiration and no corporation and that's what killed us in the end. That and the Joe-Billy thing.
>
> JOE
>
> But they don't stop floggin that horse, do they. That's why someone should line 'em up against a fuckin wall and shoot 'em. Put 'em out of our fuckin misery. Mick: Bang. Keef: Bang. Woody: Bang. Whoeverthefuck's on bass now: Bang. Charlie . . . naw, we'll spare Charlie, leave one of 'em alive to tell the tale.
>
> DIRECTOR
>
> Well now you've killed the Stones, how do you feel about your own reunion?
>
> JOE
>
> Chance to get up there remind people they're not fuckin pylons, they're not fuckin speed bumps, they got brains, wake up, use 'em.

Further changes: Billy is no longer threatening to leave for Seattle; instead, he's already in L.A. filling in on guitar for a famous funk metal band along the lines of the Chili Peppers, flirting with the bigtime sellout.

I know I swore a while back not to commercialize (i.e., further Americanize) the story, but shifting the site of Billy's dreams to L.A. from Seattle makes a lot of sense now. Let's face it, the bonfire of Seattle's musical vanities has all but burned out in the last couple years, though the scene was still a huge magnet when Turner wrote the book in 1992. For Billy to succeed in L.A. with this supergroup, he's got to be a fairly shit-hot axeman. If he's that good, HCL must have been pretty good themselves. If HCL were only a so-so local band that deservedly never got anywhere in the wider world, why bother making a movie about them? If HCL are, instead, small-time legends in the world of alternative rock, emblems of unrealized potential, a band perpetually on the brink of big things but prone to self-destruct each time a commercial breakthrough beckons, there's much more to work with dramatically. There's more I can write about the band's conflicting ideals and politics, their secrets, the hopes and fears they struggle to mask with their outward scorn (Joe's anyway) for the rewards and blandishments of music biz success. If punk prizes failure over conventional success, we'll want to know more about why a punk band chose to soldier on for ten or twelve years rather than crashing and burning in a blaze of glory after two, three, or five years, like the Pistols and so many other late 70s punk outfits.

27 June 1995

I haven't met Hugh Dillon yet. Bruce has had him read for Joe Dick with Callum Rennie, without inviting me along. Guess he didn't want my negative energy tripping Hugh up.

Bruce even sent Callum out on the road with Headstones so that he and Hugh could hang out and Callum could get a first-hand look at a rock band on tour. Actor research. Bruce now thinks it a good idea that I get in touch with Hugh and get to know him a little. Guy's got a wealth of rock 'n' roll road stories that might prove useful for the script. So I call him at home in the afternoon.

He answers the phone with an impatient bark: Yeah!

Throws me off a bit. Turns out I've woken him up, nocturnal creature that he is. I explain who I am and tell him Bruce has suggested we get together. Hugh sounds a little skeptical about this. I get the feeling that "writer" means "journalist" to him, and that "journalist" means "asshole." Still, he agrees to meet up sometime in the next few days.

Fear I won't be making the deadline at month's end. Moving tomorrow. Be happy to finish the draft by the end of next week, in time to go on another road scouting trip from Saskatchewan to Vancouver with Bruce and Miroslav.

30 June 1995

The meeting with Hugh Dillon begins at a downtown film cooperative, where Bruce has arranged for us to see his first film, *Knock Knock*, made back in 1984 or so. Callum Rennie meets us there. The idea is for us to get a notion of Bruce's previous work in the pseudodocumentary vein (*Roadkill* aside).

Hugh arrives first, wearing black cutoffs, ripped T-shirt, backwards baseball cap, shades. I introduce myself. He looks at me warily, an I've-been-burned-by-writers-before-and-you-better-not-fuck-with-me-you-asshole kind of look. It's clear I'll probably have to win him over, while he couldn't give a rat's ass if he wins me over or not. We'll be in for an interesting time of it.

Callum arrives sporting a new Steve McQueenish haircut and right away he and Hugh start in joking and slagging each other like old pals. We head in to a hot stuffy little screening room and *Knock Knock* rolls. It appears to be about Bruce himself (again, the director at the center of the picture) and his efforts to get his camera into peoples' bedrooms. Not for any prurient purpose on his part, but to exploit the prurient anxieties of his interviewees while asking them about the room's decor, the content of their closets, and the overall "feel" of their bedrooms. His quest for good interviewees leads him first to his parents' bedroom (they're quite funny and awkward), then to Washington and the White House, where his repeated requests for a tour of Ron and Nancy Reagan's bedroom are turned down. (Bruce has a letter of refusal on White House stationery to prove it.) Though this is early-Bruce film school stuff, you can see the nascent sense of social satire, the knack for self-promotion by placing himself as a director-character in his films, the guerrilla filmmaker sensibility whose attitude is part rock 'n' roll and part deconstruction. Bruce the genial provocateur as seen in more innocent times. Callum and Hugh are bored to death and make obscene finger shadows on the screen as the film plays.

After the screening Callum and Hugh are at it again, insulting each other, playing little mind games, buddying up to each other very comfortably. They've fenced off a large, mysterious area in which to develop their friendship, a place where they alone can kick back, horde secrets, develop private codes, laugh at others. Very exclusive patch of real estate by the looks of it. They'll let you in for a little visit, but they don't let you stay for long. No problem, merely observing it is giving me rich material for the script. They remind me a little of *Heavenly Creatures*, the Peter Jackson film about the two teenage girlfriends who create a magical kingdom à deux, then murder one of their mothers.

We talk for several hours about the *Hard Core* script, about Hugh's life in rock 'n' roll, about whether the script is true enough to the world he knows. Hugh explains that he wasn't sure he wanted to do the film at first after reading an early draft as well as Turner's book (though he's warming up to the new stuff). Early drafts were too mannered for him, not real enough, not cool enough. Joe Dick's West Coast punk politics were a shade too naive for his taste, a touch too earnest.

I ask what the Headstones are all about.

Just rock 'n' roll, he says, no politics.

What are you in it for? I ask.

Whatever I can get, he says.

1 July 1995

Canada Day. To the Molson Amphitheatre at Ontario Place to watch the Headstones play an outdoor event with several other bands. Crowd of about five thousand, mostly in their teens, brave the afternoon heat. A mildly embarrassing quest for backstage accreditation leads to my being handed a pass, which elicits envious looks from the fourteen-year-olds. I resolve to give it to the dorkiest little dweeb I can find the moment Headstones finish their set.

I speak briefly with Hugh before his band takes the stage. He's polite, sharp, funny, looking very much like he's going to be on his game this afternoon. I'm liking his game face. At showtime I head for the mosh pit out front for a good close look at our Joe Dick.

On stage Hugh is anything but polite, but he's definitely funny, definitely hard on the crowd. Virtually everyone moshing beneath him is a fifteen-year-old boy. They're wanking age, not drinking age, so Hugh plays up to them, making frequent dick-pulling gestures, flicking his cigarettes on them, spitting on them, farting into the mike, calling them fucking goofs. He chain-smokes through the whole show, right through his songs. He stubs cigarettes on his tongue, eats the butts. A poor role model, no doubt about it. The kids in the mosh pit nudge each other and laugh, but they love it.

I find a place to stand near the back of the spacious concrete pit, well out of harm's way. Harm, in this case, coming from Hugh's snot and spit projectiles, not from any take-yer-life-in-yer-hands moshing. A couple of songs into the show Hugh makes funny, almost apologetic faces at me, as if he's embarrassed to find himself playing some kid's birthday party. My attention wanders to the rest of the crowd.

Then Hugh barks my name into the mike.

Look back to the stage in time to see the drummer, Dale, spit into the air. The flob traces a long, high arc like a badminton birdie, coming right down into the waiting, wide open mouth of Hugh. Then Hugh spits Dale's greenie high, straight up, and catches it again in his mouth. And again. A cool punk trick he'd promised to perform when I spoke with him yesterday. The kids in the pit look at each other and go: Ewwwww! I'm mildly grossed-out myself and wonder if this will find its way into *Hard Core Logo*. Hope not. Still, our man knows how to give the kids their money's worth. As for the music, it's very solid hard rock with some tasty hooks and an alterno edge.

The show over, I give away my backstage pass (to a cute girl, so much for resolutions) and head for the exit. But a question remains: Is Hugh Dillon really capable of playing Joe Dick? Or is this the wrong question, the right one being: Can Joe Dick play Hugh Dillon?

2 July 1995

Still up to my nosehairs in this new draft. The Regina material is much stronger. Here Billy learns he's been dumped by the big L.A. band. His dream of fame and riches is left in tatters and he's trapped out here playing these Prairie toilets with the band he can't escape from, try as he might. So he freaks out. Later he buries his past differences with Joe and promises to rejoin HCL permanently, only to get word at the end that he's wanted after all by the L.A. band. At which point he walks out on Joe.

Struck out into a new direction at Bucky's farm too. Bucky tells a much abbreviated version of his sad and weird rock biz tales, but now, on finishing, he accuses Bruce (he calls him "Brice," one of Siobhan's suggestions) of being a boring hack and challenges him to do something "interesting" with the camera. Bruce takes the challenge. Bucky passes out tabs of acid to band and film crew, with a view to getting everyone in the mood to produce a little art film to liven up Bruce's otherwise "dull, journalistic" account of Hard Core's tour. What follows is a low-rent spectacle of barnyard debauchery in which the guys dress up in Bucky's old glam gear, shoot shotguns all over the place (so much for their anti-gun convictions), then round up a live goat, which Pipe chainsaws in half. Not sure how this will fly with anyone else. Works for me, though.

let's go down to hollywood

8 July 1995

Asked Hugh the other day what Headstones actually do on the road during the long hours between towns. How do they pass the time?

Watching movies, he says.

Of course that's on the band's plush tour bus, with the TVs, the VCRs, the sound system, the fridge, the sofas, and padded chairs. But what about before the tour bus, when they had to drive their own shitty van, just like Hard Core Logo?

They couldn't watch movies, so they talked about them. Played movie trivia games.

Such as?

Well, one person names a film, the next person has to name another film whose first letter starts with the last letter of the previous film.

This gave me an idea, and the result is the following scene, which takes place on the road at night between Calgary and Regina. It makes for an interestingly self-reflexive moment. It's a scene about nothing, about killing time. But it's loaded.

```
INT./EXT. THE VAN ON THE ROAD – MOVING – NIGHT

JOE at the wheel, glazed eyes staring straight
ahead. BILLY is in the seat next to him, JOHN
and PIPE sleep in back. The camera is just
behind the guys in the space between front
seats. It is raining hard outside and the
wipers are on.

                    BILLY
          Touch of Evil.
```

                    JOE
La Dolce Vita.

                    BILLY
Alphaville.

                    JOE
Lolita

                    BILLY
Alphaville ends with an "E."

                    JOE
Okay . . . um, Eraserhead.

                    BILLY
Dead Men Don't Wear Plaid.

                    JOE
'less they come from Seattle . . . Um
. . . Dead Ringers.

                    BILLY
Sssstrange . . . no . . . SSSSSpinal Tap.

Long pause as Joe thinks.

                    DIRECTOR (OS)
. . . Parenthood.

BILLY makes a derisive game-show BUZZER sound. Looks to camera.

                    BILLY
Category's cool movies. Not dumb movies.

                    JOE
            (to camera)
Loser.

                    (to Billy)
Don't you ever get sick of cool?

                    BILLY
No . . . You got one or what.

                    JOE
Okay . . . P . . . P . . . The Passenger.

                    BILLY
          (BUZZER noise again)
Starts with "T" not "P."

                    JOE
Fuck you talkin about? Passenger, The
Passenger. What's the diff?

                    BILLY
We'll let it go. Passenger . . . R . . .
Rosemary's Baby.

                    JOE
Bastard, nothin good starts with a "Y"
. . . Yyyyyyyentl . . .

BILLY does the BUZZER again.

                    JOE
. . . Youngblood . . .
          (Billy's BUZZER)
Yyyyyoung and Restless.

                    BILLY
That's a soap.

                    JOE
Yabadabadoo . . . You Suck . . .

Yyyyyesterday's Lunch . . . Young at Heart!

                BILLY

What's that?

                JOE

Frank Sinatra, Doris Day. Frank's a depressed lounge singer. Doris feels sorry for him and marries him. Frank doesn't think he deserves her love so he cracks up his car on purpose.

                BILLY

Does he die?

                JOE

Naw, ends up back with Doris.

                BILLY
                (BUZZER noise)

Totally uncool.

                JOE

I'm too tired to fuckin think.

                BILLY

Still okay for driving?

                JOE

Yeah.

JOE blinking at the road ahead. ZOOM onto the road ahead, the white line. The van begins to veer around on it a bit.

                BILLY

Joe?

─────────── let's go down to hollywood ───────────

                         JOE
    I'm fine!

BILLY glances to camera.

Thought it a good idea to get the *Spinal Tap* issue right into the open here. Acknowledge the ancestor, as it were. The other issue is romantic: Joe's inability to think of a cool film that starts with a Y (as in "Why") leads him to choose a 1950s Technicolor romance about a self-destructive musician who goes to the brink of death for love, but is delivered unto a happy ending with Doris Day (a weirdly idealized Billy Tallent). Billy's scorn for *Young at Heart* warns Joe not to expect any happy ending to his renewed "courtship."

Following up on this romance theme, I dropped a bomb into one of John's fragile monologues, suggesting that the real source of the Joe-Billy tension lies in the fact that Joe once anally raped Billy, creating what the critics will doubtless call a tense homoerotic subtext. John's disclosure of Joe and Billy's dark secret might be motivated by a desire to pull down the two band leaders to avenge his own years of obscurity as "John the bass player." Definitely reveals a dangerous tactlessness which schizophrenic John thinks of as honesty. Whether it's true in the story or not doesn't really matter at this stage. The fact that it might be is more than enough to charge up the dramatic tension.

Looks like I'll be finished with this pass through the script in time to take that trip out West. Looking forward to it.

10 July 1995

So I finish the draft. It's Sunday morning. Plane leaves for the Prairies late this afternoon. First, a script meeting at Frizzell's well-appointed penthouse high above the metropolis. I arrive to find John, Christine, and Brian, but no Bruce. We start the meeting without him.

Brief round of praise for the improvements. I relax, gratified. Then slowly, inevitably, the criticisms trickle forth: the goat slaying at Bucky's is okay, but added to Joe and Billy's homosexual backstory, it's sure to scare off American investors. There still needs to be a bigger build to the end where the band split up. The ending seems forced and artificial. The critique gets more and more detailed and serious as everyone gathers steam (law of nature: sustained criticism comes much more easily to people than sustained praise). I sit there nodding, smiling, pretending to take notes, my heart sinking by the minute.

Where is Bruce!? Why isn't he here when I need him to back me up?

Frizzell, Brian, and Christine have covered all their notes to their satisfaction when Bruce finally arrives with his packed bags, ready for the road trip. We gloss over the points again for his benefit, and Bruce's surreptitious look suggests that I take much of the criticism with a grain of salt, that much of it is motivated by producer fear. But when things wrap up, Bruce shrugs and smiles when the others suggest that I sit tight here in Toronto and grind out another draft more pleasing to potential investors. And can I possibly have it finished in another two weeks?

Back home Siobhan says, aren't you going out of town today? I shake my head, sit down, and begin at the beginning once more.

14 July 1995

Shit week. There's an unholy heat wave parked over Toronto and everywhere you go people trudge along with the wilted looks of jungle soldiers under heavy packs. Put in a lot of time writing in the War Room at Shadow Shows partly because the office is cooler than my work room at home, but also to be near Frizzell who is there putting together *The Rez* series. From time to time Frizzell looks over my shoulder, rewards me with an ooo, very good, punishes me with a hmm, don't know about that. He makes some good suggestions and some lousy ones. But at least the pace is quick and the constant feedback a comfort after spending much of the last year working alone.

We spend a lot of time talking about what is "likely" in documentary filmmaking, about the logic of privacy, of what people do and don't do (or say) on camera. I'm trying to make sure there's an offhand, naturalistic, accidental feel to the drama, to the way information is captured by the camera. The form imposes some frustrating limitations, but with the form foregrounded like this, it also creates an opportunity to explore documentary filmmaking and the motivations of documentary filmmakers. Nearly every scene addresses the presence of the camera in some way, implicitly or explicitly. Naturally there are dramatic beats, plot points, and reversals as in most classically structured screenplays, but they are disguised here under a layer of planned naturalism. If Bruce can follow this accidental logic in production, the audience will not spend much time thinking about the logic of the documentary camera getting reaction shots and so on.

In the middle of one of these sessions at the office, Bruce calls from somewhere in Alberta. The scouting trip with Christine and Miro is going well, he says, but now he's thinking the documentary style we've been working in isn't going to work at all.

It's another one of those moments.

hard core roadshow

Bruce says that Miroslav, visual guy that he is, can't see the point of shooting documentary-style out in the majestic West. Be a waste of the film's "cinematic potential," he says. Miro is thinking of giving the picture a more epic visual sweep and he has Bruce convinced that he's right, that scrapping the docu shtick and rewriting the script as straight drama is the way to go.

Well he's got me convinced that smashing the phone into little pieces is the way to go. I explain that great strides are being made with the current direction and that too much time and work have gone into it to throw it out now. And anyway, what's a cameraman doing calling the creative shots at this stage? Frizzell senses that something's wrong, gets on the line, listens to Bruce's thoughts. Then tells Bruce to forget it. He hangs up, looks at me, and says not to worry about it.

Try to get back to work, but my blood's hit the boiling point. Goddammit, I knew something like this would happen if they went out West without me. Someone suggests that it's all just a process that Bruce has to go through to figure out "what he wants to do." I pine for the day when I'll direct my own films, vulnerable to the failings of no one's whims but my own.

Later I write a moment where Pipefitter turns on Bruce and the camera crew, asking Bruce who the hell he thinks he is, calling him a parasite, telling him his other so-called road movies suck, boasting that Hard Core Logo will be around a lot longer than Bruce will. Feels good writing it, though on reading it later I feel small and ashamed. Yet Frizzell howls when I show it to him, and even suggests adding a couple more vicious lines.*

---

* Bruce, brave soul, later finds it hilarious and Bernie Coulson performs the scene powerfully in production.

18 July 1995

The inadequacy of pictures as a primary vehicle for telling stories. In spite of feeling like I may be doing some of my best work as a screenwriter, right here and now, I am sick of writing screenplays. Sick to death of them.

Screenwriting is a blighted ghetto, a literary no-man's-land. Screenwriting serves a medium which does not prize language,

Fuck screenwriting, let's walk.

poetry, wordplay, or conversation. While there's usually a need to write dialogue (consider it a gift if you can find it done decently at the movies), talk is considered a mere footnote to image. Pictures have all the power. Pictures get all the babes. Still, it is words, properly arranged, that seduce, enchant, inspire, educate in a more lasting way than transient pictures. People generally leave films quoting not the most memorable images, but the most memorable lines. Of course, audiences are viewers, not readers, and they tend not to marvel at the wit and wisdom of the utterly anonymous writer whose name flashed briefly on the screen, but at the wit and wisdom of the actor who speaks this nobody's words.

Wrote a new scene for John where he burns his diary after Pipe reads it aloud. He faces the camera as it burns, tells Bruce with no small amount of irony and bitterness that "words come and go, but pictures never die." I find more and more of the uneasy discourse between the band and the film crew in the script springs from my own anger with the craft of screenwriting. Anger which I tend to take out on my personal punching bag, the fictional Bruce. Sublimation doesn't get any more transparent than this.

23 July 1995

My my hey hey, been on this ride for a year and a day.

24 July 1995

News of drastic government cutbacks here in Ontario. Which portend consequences for us. I call Brian Dennis, who confirms that we may well be dead in the water. For the moment, at least.

Our new populist Conservative premier is the obnoxiously self-satisfied glad-handing back-slapping business-loving social spending and public-sector-hating small-town golf pro-turned-New-Right-zealot, Mike Harris. Mike has vowed to eliminate the deficit. If a few government-funded films don't get made, it's no big deal. But Mike's anti-spending jihad includes cuts to welfare, health care, education, women's shelters, anyone young, disenfranchised, marginalized, or creative. His government has pledged to "stop the bleeding" by hacking at everything in sight. Even government investment programs are being lopped off, and this is where we've been hit: just announced is a freeze on $6.5 million of the OFDC's $10.5 million annual budget. As we have not quite got around to signing our production funding contracts with the OFDC (who are verbally committed to the project and have already financed a large portion of script development), we are about to see a large chunk of money, nearly a third of the film's budget, disappear. Just like that.

What can we do about this? Two things. With Christine on board as producer, we can exploit her B.C. residency status and the film's B.C. setting to apply to B.C. Film (B.C.'s version of the OFDC) for the money we've just lost. They've only just begun whispering about cutbacks out in NDP-run B.C., and the reality won't be upon them for some time yet. We could well qualify for their funding, as long as virtually all the below-the-line personnel are B.C. residents.

The second thing we might do if we're really brave, is test the waters in L.A. and see if there are any Americans interested in throwing money into this film. So there's really no need to panic. Is there? Well . . . yes. We still don't have production financing from Telefilm, and their green light has not been given by any means. What exactly do we have, if not money? A script, sort of. A director, a couple of producers, most of a cast, and some music. All of which signify nothing without money. Which is why this is called the film business.

27 July 1995

Much outrage and frustration in recent entries. All of it true to the moment. Most of it, in retrospect, overwrought. Especially now that I've finished the draft, delivered it to Bruce, and made my peace with screenwriting once more. I love what I do. Bruce is my pal and I love working with him. Feel good about the world in general. Mind you, my comments about Mike Harris still stand.

Some interesting news on the financing front. Citytv (MuchMusic, Bravo, etc.) have officially entered the picture as investors. A pre-sale is also in the works with a German distributor called TIME. On top of this, copies of the new script have been sent out to Christine, who is now in L.A. with Karen Powell, a Vancouver entertainment lawyer who is going to be our associate producer. In the course of shopping the latest draft, they've run into a potential investor named Walter Shenson. All I've heard about Walter is that he's the guy who produced *A Hard Day's Night* and *Help!* Be hilarious if our little punk picture is rescued from financing limbo and exec produced by the man who made the Beatles' movies.

30 July 1995

Drop in at the office to hear that some executive at a major company in L.A. loves the script and would consider solving all our financial problems . . . but the goat slaughter during the acid sequence has to go. Guy's an animal rights activist and can't abide the thought of nonhuman blood being spilled in his movies. Brian votes we lose the goat scene and get on with it. Bruce says sure, first it's the goat, then what? One long slippery slope of compromise. You make one change to please the suits, they walk all over you and you lose control of the movie. The goat stays, he says stubbornly.

So the goat is more than a gratuitous blood sacrifice in the film. It's becoming a symbol of the struggle to make an independent film. It's becoming a rallying point. Porteous is in town and comes over. I show him the scene on my

let's go down to hollywood

computer screen. "Wrong and strong," he says. Beats correct and weak, fate of oh so many films in this country.

3 August 1995

Walter Shenson and his partners are in for half a mill! He's officially an exec producer. We're being produced by the guy who produced the Beatles' movies. A totally unexpected turn of events. Seems he's connected to a Chicago-based video distributor who put out the Beatles' films (as well as — this inspires confidence — *Henry: Portrait of a Serial Killer*), and the reason the Chicago people are in is that they've just made a deal to pre-buy U.S. video rights to *Hard Core*. Can't wait to meet Walter, pump him for John Lennon stories. Bruce is thrilled. We talk about how the ads will run: "From the producer of *A Hard Day's Night* . . . It's . . . HARD CORE LOGO!" And as far as Walter is concerned, the goat can stay.

It's very exciting, hearing about all these wheelings and dealings in far-off places with my script as the key object of barter. A languid moment of self-satisfaction, then a chilling nightmare image flashes across my mind: Mike Harris stands in the Ontario legislature shouting down the Opposition's culture critic in defense of his arts cuts, "Hey just look at this *Hard Core Logo* movie. After it lost provincial funding the producers made like entrepreneurs, got off their lazy duffs, went out into the real world, and raised private sector money. That's what the Common Sense Revolution is all about!" It's like a long set of nails raking down an inner chalkboard.

8 August 1995

Feedback. Thanks to a couple of high-minded and unforgiving readers' reports from Telefilm, production funding won't be in the cards for the latest draft, despite commitments from private sources. One report, an eight-page manifesto about Road Narratives, Beautiful Losers, and Failed Canadiana, trashes my script for the crime of not being *Highway 61*.

In search of a fresh perspective, I e-mail the script to David Griffith, my erstwhile writing partner who lives in Scotland. We've been carrying on an international collaboration for a few years on a variety of projects. Dave still hasn't seen the *HCL* script. I've been holding off, waiting until it's good enough for his eyes. I ask him for a brutally frank response.

He sends me a lengthy essay which includes the best feedback from anyone so far. Dave's far too cool for brutal frankness; instead he tactfully suggests a few minor adjustments to boost the script's forward thrust. One of these is brilliant and it changes everything: that the benefit show itself should be a scam, that Bucky never really was shot, Joe Dick has built this big lie and organized the benefit solely to entice Billy back to Canada, back into the band where Joe spent his happiest years. Gives Joe a fresh diabolical aspect, a cunning Satan in *Paradise Lost* dimension. Should fit Hugh Dillon like a kid glove.

Bruce comes over and we shut ourselves in my work room to discuss a new set of script notes for the obdurate Telefilm people. I explain Dave's suggestion and we excitedly talk through its implications. I begin writing the script notes, adding in new twists and turns to the storyline: the band's money is stolen by hookers Joe parties with in Regina, a big fight among band members is moved from near the end to before the visit to Bucky's place, the band stay at a campground after Saskatoon and stumble into a gang of Nazi skinheads, who chase the band, beat the shit out of filmmaker Bruce, then shave his head. When Joe is accused in Edmonton of faking the benefit concert, Billy backs him saying, "We saw Bucky, he's in a wheelchair, we touched his stump." When filmmaker Bruce discovers the entire odyssey is based on Joe's scam, he starts to take it out on the band. There's a new perversity, a brio, a bravado, to the storyline. By the time we're finished, my notes are in fact a new ten-page outline for a souped-up *Hard Core Logo*, a film that runs on a mixture of love and lies.

We drop this off at Shadow Shows with Brian and Frizzell, then meet Hugh Dillon for dinner and drinks. Mid-evening I call Brian from the restaurant to see if he and John have read the notes. They have. We need to talk tomorrow, Brian says, but won't elaborate about whether he and John liked the changes or not. Doesn't sound good to me. Back at the table through several rounds of drinks, Bruce, Hugh, and I discuss the new changes and ideas. Hugh is excited, loves the idea of the scam, the big lie, and asks for more of this kind of detail for his character.

Later, Hugh and I leave Bruce and move on to the Clearspot on College Street. We haven't really had the chance to talk alone yet and Hugh wants to do some more serious drinking and shit-shooting. Beers are ordered. There's a lull in the talk until we sit. Then Hugh leans aggressively over and says he's heard that I don't think he's right for the role of Joe Dick. So what's my fucking problem anyway?

Boom. There it is. He's locked into my eyes, waiting for a straight answer. I have two choices: deny I ever had a problem with casting him, or defend my opinion. I go for the latter, explaining that I didn't think he was right at first, based on what I'd seen of him in *Dance Me Outside*. He's being called on here to carry a whole movie, and no one's seen enough of his acting to know whether he can pull it off. Now I'm getting to know him, I explain, and can see that he's a natural performer pretty well every minute of the day, so I'm much less worried.

This seems to bury the issue and we get on with the drinking and telling of stories from our lives. Hugh's form a rather proud litany of benders, run-ins with gun-toting drug dealers, fights and arguments with music business assholes, cool things he's said and done on stage (all grist for my mill). Mine are surprisingly similar, except the drug dealers weren't toting guns and I've never gotten up to much on stage. We hit the street long after the bar closes and part ways as buddies. Not Callum-Hugh type buddies, mind you, but something that sends me home feeling validated nonetheless.

9 August 1995

To Shadow Shows with a pounding head and expecting the worst. Bruce, Brian, Frizzell, and I sit in the War Room. Everyone sparks a butt. It ain't a creative meeting unless everyone's smoking.

Frizzell gets the ball rolling: This, he says, is more than a set of script notes. This is an outline for an entirely different film. Brian chips in his agreement. I'm thinking that we must have fucked up somehow, but no, they love the changes.

There is a snag, however: it's so much better, Frizzell says, that we should not submit the previous draft with this outline to Telefilm's Vancouver office (Christine has suggested we deal with Vancouver exclusively, bypassing the more truculent Toronto office), but the next draft, based on the new outline. This will probably take not one week to complete, but two or three. It will push back our production date by as much as a month, possibly into October. Weather could be a problem. The interior of B.C. and Alberta, where we will be shooting road sequences, will be snowbound by November.

I wonder why we can't simply submit the present draft and these script notes so Telefilm will know where we're going to end up on the script front. But Brian and John are adamant that we "put our best foot forward."

So that's that. Churn the next draft out. So much for the rest of the summer. Here comes another marathon at the computer, locked indoors, away from my vacationing playgoing film-watching rollerblading cycling swimming cottaging partying bar-hopping barbecuing summer enjoying friends. Siobhan decides to enjoy what she can of it on her own. She's heading off to California to visit her mother for a couple of weeks, her theory being that I won't notice her absence anyway.

16 August 1995

Working on my own this time, with no story editor to talk to, as Frizzell is gearing up *The Rez* for production this fall. I drop by Shadow Shows because Bruce has some videotapes of actors to show me for the role of John. Several are good, but one really sticks out: an actor named John Pyper-Ferguson, whom Bruce met recently while directing an episode of *Lonesome Dove* in Alberta. The role of John is much more complex now than he was in the earliest drafts, and we need an actor who can go from naive sweetness to psychotic rage and back, without looking foolish. Pyper-Ferguson plays vulnerable psychos from end to end on his demo reel and he looks perfect. But he'll have to cut his Charles Manson hippie hair.

And then there were four: our sweet psycho, John Pyper-Ferguson.

20 August 1995

Continuing work on the script. In the office an unending buzz of talk about Telefilm, Walter Shenson's people, potential start dates for the film, potential delays. Names of bureaucrats out West that I've never heard of are suddenly on everyone's lips. New names, same old story as far as I can tell.

In our spare time Bruce and I are studying acting together. Bruce has arranged a private workshop for us with Daniel Brooks at the Tarragon Theatre. In my case, I'm looking for extra insight into how actors create character, how they modulate behavior, how they interact with other characters. For Bruce the idea is to get into thinking like an actor, to prepare himself to elicit the best performances he possibly can out of our ensemble cast. We workshop the perversely appropriate *True West* by Sam Shepard. Bruce plays Lee, the older brother, a wayward drifter and small-time crook. I play younger brother Austin, the preppy hack screenwriter. Bruce is having more fun with his role than I am with mine.

28 August 1995

The new draft is done. I have no idea how many times I've written words to this effect. Several. Anyway, this should be the one. Be surprised if it doesn't finally get us the money. Wrote yet another set of notes for the Vancouver Telefilm people to justify the latest changes, and off they've gone. We are dealing now with different development officers and readers, and we're hoping for a more sympathetic response from the office in the city where we're actually planning to shoot the film. Maybe people out there will be a little less judgmental about what kind of films they want Bruce McDonald to be making. Maybe they won't give a damn as long as it's good.

29 August 1995

Siobhan calls with interesting news from California where she's been visiting her mother for a couple of weeks. She's late, she says. As in, you know . . . *late*.

It is only long after the call, and long after the news has sunk in as a complication, an unfair encroachment into a sanctified creative bubble, that I realize how far gone I am with this screenwriting obsession. The rest of the day is a vortex of questions. Am I ready for kids? Is she? Are we? How much more ready had we wanted to be before reaching this formerly hypothetical but now very real moment? How much more financially stable or successful were we supposed to be before it would be "convenient" to hear the pitter-patter of little feet? How much more had I hoped to accomplish before this? How much more had Siobhan? How did this one get past the sentries anyway?

7 September 1995

Siobhan's back. It's confirmed: we are to be parents. My feelings about the news in chronological order: shock, fear, denial, resistance, uncertainty, compassion, fear again, worry, curiosity, interest, intimacy, a twinge of excitement, warm coziness all over, acceptance, peace, belonging, a sense of continuity, passion, intense love, an outpouring of affection for the whole world, thralldom, and today, hysterical excitement. There are days when you have to admit that life is better than movies, love is better than glory.

*

My life hasn't been all *HCL*. Other things I've done over the last year: with Dave, via e-mail, moved ahead on *Brutally, Frank* and rewrote *Gotterdammerung*. With the Russian director Mark Ioussefov, I reworked a feature script called *Delusion*. This is still in development with Telefilm. I worked with a couple of actors, Dean Paras and Stefan Brogren, on a rewrite of their comedy, *European Supermodel*. Added dozens of story ideas to the story idea file. Started sketching out another novel I'll probably never write. Lined up an agent. Moved a couple of times. Walked the dog. Made new friends. Went to funerals and weddings. Went to parties, plays, films, openings, closings, concerts, readings, bars. Took in Jays games. Took up exercise, dropped it under work pressure. Quit smoking. Started again. Quit again. Started again. Stared out the window. Read a fair bit, Montaigne in particular (primo style manual for personal essayists and diarists — for all the good it's done me here). Had fun. Had arguments. Had breakfast, lunch, and dinner. Had unprotected sex once, evidently.

8 September 1995

At work polishing the script when I hear about trouble out West. There's been some confusion about the new script, some of which can be chalked up to communication problems between Bruce's and Christine's offices. Somehow in the shuffle Telefilm's Vancouver office has been given the wrong draft of the script — the old one, not the new one. I take it that Christine thought they had the new one, only to learn otherwise the other day. So in goes the new version. More complications as Telefilm now belatedly evaluates the current draft. More delays. More waiting.

9 September 1995

David Griffith is in town for the festival and for more work on *Brutally, Frank*. But first I press-gang him into helping me with *HCL* and he comes up with some excellent suggestions for the middle and end of the script.

He wonders why I persist in following the notion from the book that the band's Winnipeg gig has been canceled. The film needs action and movement, so rather than leaving the band with nothing to do for two or three days in Saskatchewan, why not actually send them all the way to Winnipeg, where they find out that the club they've been booked into has been closed down by the city for some liquor code violation? This makes the journey longer and adds yet another picaresque insult to the piled-up injuries. Dave also suggests rearranging the placement of about three scenes at the end. Now things are looking really sharp. Nice to have fresh eyes on a piece of work so late in the game; they can spot things you've long since ceased to see, having labored over them at such close range for so many months.

*

We stop in at Shadow Shows before catching a film, as I want to introduce Dave to the people I'm working with in this city. We run into John Frizzell and Don McKellar on the way in. I introduce Dave and ask Frizzell if he's heard any word on the script from Telefilm's B.C. office (he gives the impression of being in constant contact with the powers that be). He says he hasn't but suggests the current delay lies in Telefilm's likely problems with — here's a close paraphrase — a weak script about four emotionally stunted losers who can't talk to each other. John and Don float out the door to a screening. On the way up the stairs Dave says, "Ouch."

*

We see Callum Rennie at a festival party. He's pissed about the lags, snags, and delays on *Hard Core*, tells me he hasn't heard anything, doesn't like the way he's been left hanging. No one's even made a formal offer for his services in the film yet. I tell him they probably can't send him a contract until the money's in the bag, and the money ain't in the bag yet. A photographer comes and pulls Callum away. He immediately kills his frown, puts on his game face, and gives the camera several of the smiles that could easily make him famous some day.

*

Siobhan leaves the festival party trail to Dave and me. She's too cool, too smart, and too busy to hang out in crowds of people who are looking for ways to make use of each other.

Bump into Bruce and ask him why he's missing all these film festival parties Dave and I have been hitting with such dogged regularity. He says festival parties are overloaded with bottom feeders. Oh.

17 September 1995

Stop in at Shadow Shows. Brian is jubilant: an end to the delays out West. At last we've been given the green light from the creative office at Telefilm.

Brian says that with the creative go the film is as good as made. All we have to wait for is the approval from Telefilm's business end after the next national meeting of offices in Vancouver, Toronto, Montreal, and Halifax. A mere formality, Brian says. It's going to happen. *Hard Core Logo* is finally going to be made. I know I should be completely thrilled, exhilarated, over the moon, etc., but all I really feel right now is relief.

2 October 1995

Bruce calls from Vancouver. He's already out there to prep the film. I ask him when I'm to come out for rehearsals. He's not sure. Suggests I be ready to go at a moment's notice. He and Christine have a meeting with the business people at Telefilm tomorrow, he says. I assume they'll wrap up the financing dance with the Chicago people and cut the cheque. Bruce is sure the deal's in the bag, though he's not dishing too many details here. When I press with more pointed questions about our status, he just says it'll all work out fine.

But when I talk to Christine I get the feeling the sky could fall on this thing any minute. Her view is that nothing is settled, that there's nothing to be too confident about. It is difficult to find the truth of the matter between the director's habitual optimism and the producer's habitual anxiety. Whatever the spin, it's clear there are mysterious financial and legal details to be attended to, and no one is willing to attach a firm start date to the film.

6 October 1995

No word from Bruce for a few days now and there's this horrible feeling that all is not well. Call the production office in Vancouver and get Christine. The horrible feeling is justified: she's in a panic. Turns out, contrary to what I've thought for three weeks, that *Hard Core* is not yet officially a "go" project at Telefilm Canada. The Telefilm business people are haggling over a definition of "investor" with our Chicago moneymen, whom Telefilm considers to be distributors, not investors in line to recoup money from the same stream as Telefilm themselves.

It's all very complicated, a skirmish down in the fine print, and everyone's jumping through hoops trying to figure it out. Here we are, two weeks away from the first day of photography and our primary investors seem to be threatening to kill the film for fear of finding themselves in a less favored recoupment position than the other guy. For future reference, I'll do well to remember that those with the bucks to invest in films are often more interested in the structure of the deal than in the work itself.

8 October 1995

Bruce calls, says that Telefilm's business office has finally given us the green light. We're a "go" project at last.

Seems all is being sorted out. After all these fits and starts and stops, we're doing it, we're finally going to make this

———————— let's go down to hollywood ————————

movie. A relief. I originally told people I'd be going West for the production in April or so. As the months thudded by the date was pushed further and further back to the point where no one seemed to believe there really was going to be any movie. At last, something firm to tell people.

13 October 1995

Ticket's booked for Monday the 16th. I'll be on the same flight as Hugh and Miroslav. The movie starts production on the 21st. I'll be going to Vancouver for more than rehearsals, I'll be there through the entire production period. The producers keep telling me that I should consider myself lucky, that writers are never on the set. I can think of dozens of productions where writers were on the set from start to finish. With something as naturalistic as *Hard Core Logo*, my being there will mean I can rewrite moments on the set to take advantage of whatever comes up in the filming process.

Meanwhile news of further, endless meetings between our producers, Telefilm, and Walter's people from Chicago. Probably found some new clauses to haggle over. Bruce says this sort of thing happens all the time in independent film, where people wait til the last minute to pull some stunt and try for a better recoupment deal. Where does this leave things? As a Hollywood guy might put it, they're set, but not set-set.

15 October 1995

Get in to find a message from Bruce: "Call me, I'm not sure if we're starting on the 21st." Jesus, here we go.

Call the production office in Vancouver. Bruce is not there; he's leaving for the airport, catching a flight to L.A. If I hurry I might still be able to get him at the hotel.

Call the hotel. Bruce answers, breathless, heading for the door and his flight, he hasn't got much time. I ask what's going on, what's wrong. There's more dancing left to do, he says, thanks to a last minute financing snag. He hopes to sort it out in L.A. Knowing that I'm meeting with Hugh and Callum tonight, Bruce simply asks me to tell Callum that he's going south to fight to keep him in the movie. Not sure what this means. Bruce won't elaborate. He confirms that there might be a little delay, tells me to sit tight. I call Christine in Vancouver but she's not in. I leave a message asking for clarification about this little delay.

I meet with Hugh and Callum at Peter Moore's recording studio where Hugh is laying vocal tracks onto the already recorded *HCL* music. As Callum lets me in, I can hear Hugh shrieking out vocals from the studio in back, his voice disembodied from any music. It's Absolut Hugh, pure naked aggression, throat-shredding vocals, makes your hair stand on end. The song is "Something's Gonna Die Tonight" and I realize that if this guy can act like he sings he'll tear up the screen.

When the session is over, Hugh and Peter emerge from the studio, very happy with their work together. Hugh has shaved the sides of his dome and now sports a fat mohawk. He wonders if this is a good Joe Dick look. I'm not sure. Strikes me as a bit retro, but then again, why not? It's a perfect Joe Dick look. Joe the punk torch bearer.

The four of us listen to the tracks through. Same music Swamp Baby recorded, but Hugh's vocals have put some hair on its chest. These toons rock. For the first time, I realize that Hard Core Logo really are a great sounding band, that people will buy into the myth we're creating about them. Hugh and Peter can't wait for Bruce to hear them.

I explain Bruce's alarming news, relaying to Callum what Bruce had said about fighting to keep him in the picture, that there may be a delay. Callum is not, shall we say, thrilled to hear about it. He has a commitment to appear in the series *My Life as a Dog*. A delay could cause a scheduling conflict, which could lead to us losing Callum altogether. We sit around complaining about the odd and incomprehensible problems that persist on the business/financial/scheduling end of the project. Then we decide to make the most of the evening and get down to some work.

We go through the script at the Midtown on College, searching for last-minute improvements. Hugh explains that there are a number of lines that he "would never say." Not a problem, I tell him, since Joe Dick is saying them and not him. But Hugh is stubbornly attached to his own version of his character's authenticity, and after two hours we've negotiated our way through maybe ten script pages, as Hugh likes to stop and justify every suggested word change with a long context-setting explanation of its origin in his own life. Hugh keeps a fat mental file of all the sassy zinger lines, snappy comebacks, and withering put-downs that have tripped out of his mouth over his years of soldiering on the rock 'n' roll battlefield. I start out penciling in some of these suggestions, but eventually give up when it occurs to me that the changes are minor and trivial, that the sense of the dialogue will still hit the screen intact, whatever Hugh's delivery happens to be.

When Hugh goes to the washroom, Callum tells me he thinks this is good exercise for Hugh, it'll help him "own" his character more fully. Unfortunately, the bar closes before I can get to Callum's thoughts. When we part at two in the morning, Hugh promises to swing by in the limo to pick me up tomorrow afternoon at five for the drive to the airport. For his part, Callum has to return to Winnipeg for a few days' work on *My Life as a Dog*. He'll join us in Vancouver just before production starts, whenever that may be now.

Back home, there's a message waiting from Christine and her tone freaks me out. I call her in Vancouver and out comes the story Bruce wouldn't tell me: disaster has struck, the unthinkable has happened. Instead of being carried over the threshold, *HCL* has been bent over the porch rail and fisted. We're fucked, we're dead in the water, it's game over, baby.

Apparently the Chicago money and Telefilm couldn't come to terms in the end over their various contractual beefs, so the Chicago money has gone south, taking their half a mill with them. We're no longer talking about some "little delay" to the start of production, but outright cancellation. Bruce is now in L.A. to beg for money from anyone who'll listen.

Christine continues, and every word is a torture: maybe we'll make the film in the spring when we can find more money. Maybe it'll never get made. Won't be the first film to be killed at the eleventh hour. She wouldn't bother flying out if she were me, she says bluntly. Of course, if I don't want to waste a plane ticket I can always come out and visit my mother for a few days.

I hang up and sit there feeling the knot in my stomach tightening.

16 October 1995

Hugh calls at nine this morning for an update on last night's unnerving news from Vancouver. I tell him the story Christine related in the middle of the night. He freaks out, hangs up.

A while later he calls back. He's spoken to Christine, heard the news for himself. He says he's been psyched for weeks to

―――――――――― let's go down to hollywood ――――――――――

do this film and he'll be fucked if he's going to see it die now. He says he can't wait until five in the afternoon to get to the airport, he's calling the limo right fucking now and catching the next flight to Vancouver. As if leaving now is going to help the film get made. His rationale is simple: he's had it set in his mind that he's going out there to kick ass in this movie. So goddammit, if he's gotta kick some ass to get the movie made, he's gonna do it. He's an impulsive rock 'n' roller, and when he wants something he wants it now.

Hugh says I too can be a rock 'n' roller and he'll pick me up in the limo in like half an hour, or I can be a college boy fag and sit around all day waiting for my scheduled flight. I still haven't made up my mind to go, tell him I've got stuff to do and won't be ready to leave till the end of the day. If at all.

Call Keith Porteous, give him the scoop and ask what he'd do in my shoes. Wise man that he is, he advises me to get on the plane this afternoon for karmic reasons. Proceed as if you're making the film, he says. He reminds me about Destiny and advises me not to panic. He's been right so far. Except for the part about sitting with the popcorn in the theater watching *Hard Core Logo* in a year. It's already been fourteen months since he said that.

Spend the day packing, making and taking calls, hiding the more obscene jottings and scene fragments that litter my workspace. At four Siobhan and I say our good-byes for either six days or six weeks. Hard to say which. I've packed light. The pessimist in me. Grab my bag, streetcar to the subway station. Take the subway many stops out to Islington station. Then it's on to one of those Airport Express buses. If this was flying time, I'd be over Calgary by now. And to think that I could have been a true rock 'n' roller first thing this morning and breezed out here in a plush limo with the star.

It's a miserable flight, and everything I hear, see, and taste seems to portend disaster. Somewhere over the Great Lakes Van Morrison comes onto the Canadian Airlines rock channel singing the words, "My mama told me there'd be days like this." Van's mama might have; mine didn't. She never told me that investor conflicts over recoupment positioning could kill your first film a week before it's scheduled to go into production.

The death of the film will lead to some immediate problems for me. I'm down to my last five hundred bucks. If there's no first day of principal photography, there is no final payment for my script and I will be in serious financial shit. Worst case scenario: *Hard Core* dies on the vine; I can't make my rent at the end of the month; I, my pregnant spouse, and my loyal beagle will be thrown out onto the street. I'll have to take the first job I can find telemarketing, taxi driving, pedicab pulling, delivering junk mail, removing asbestos. Might even give workfare a crack. Day-glo tunic, coveralls, broom, dustpan, sweeping the sidewalks at Bloor and Yonge, right below the Telefilm office. Or go the small-time entrepreneurial distance and become a street-corner squeegee punk, duking it out with all the other punks for the spare change of irate drivers.

The drink trolley mercifully arrives and I buy four mini-bottles of scotch. Just remembered that today is my birthday. It's the least of my worries . . . turning nineteen and all. My birthday horoscope in the *Globe and Mail*: "A new admirer wants to get together with you. Long distance travel could be involved. An almost forgotten investment could pay off better than projected." Hmmm.

*

let's go down to hollywood

Nine o'clock and raining as the plane touches down in Vancouver. I am greeted at the gate by this funky chick in jeans and leather jacket, holding up a scrap of paper with my name scrawled on it, the thing they do for celebs and mail-order brides arriving from far-flung places. Turns out this is Karen Powell, LL.B., our associate producer. She tells me Bruce is still in L.A., nothing's settled.

We go directly to our assistant director's loft, where a dinner party is in full swing and a sort of gallows humor prevails. The drinks are going down hard and fast. There's a sarcastic toast to our former American investors. Hugh is here, looking very much at home. So is Christine, looking knackered but nothing like the wreck I was expecting after our phone call.

I meet Rachel Leiterman, our assistant director, who is relaxed and good humored and sort of giggling and dancing around the place. I meet the actor John Pyper-Ferguson, who will play John if the film gets made. An interesting cat. Wears this wide-brimmed green leather sort of bowler hat. Still has the long hair and the mustache. There's something of the cowboy about him and something of a hippie. His friends call him Pyper. Right away he calls me "brother." As in, "Hey, brother, howzit goin?" He's in a great mood. In all, everyone's a hell of a lot more relaxed than I am.

After dinner, Pyper, Hugh, and I hit the Railway for last call. Chance to see how these two get along. Doesn't take long to find out. We get beers, take seats, and Hugh out and horks in Pyper's face. His little way of establishing who fits where in the pecking order. Hugh says this is how it goes in his own band, might as well be the same here, seeing as he's the "leader" and all. Pyper takes it in stride, wipes the spit, even lends Hugh forty bucks. Then, to show that fair's fair, Hugh opens his mouth wide and demands that Pyper spit in it. Which Pyper resists for a few minutes until Hugh basically orders him to spit. John spits, hits Hugh on the nose. Close enough. Now there's a basis for a relationship.

When they announce last call, Pyper packs it in and the two wired Torontonians continue into the night. We hook up with some nightclub guys Hugh knows from playing here with the Headstones. More drinks. Then it's off to someone's apartment for further consumption of one thing and another. Then it's starting to get light out, then it's suddenly nine in the morning local time. Noon for me. Back to the hotel where I pass out. Hugh continues partying til noon local time, three for him. The boy has stamina. Then again, he has more practice at this than most.

17 October 1995

Phone wakes me in the afternoon. It's Bruce down at the production office, back from L.A. Suggests I get my ass on down there.

Stumble out of bed, gauge my surroundings. I'm in a new hotel called the Rosedale, at Robson and Hamilton in the eastern end of downtown Vancouver. Two bedroom suite with living/dining room, kitchenette, matching lacquered tables and chairs, bland from end to end and home for the next few days or weeks, depending on how things go. It's not all mine of course. Bruce has kindly invited me to stay with him here since there's no budget provision for my accommodation as there is for other out-of-town personnel.

Look out the window to find shades of a creeping world-class cityitis, a disease afflicting ambitious mid-sized cities, leading to delusions of grandeur. Across the street is the new public library, designed to evoke the classical grandeur of Rome's Coliseum, combined with the monumental upward thrust of the Tower of Babel. A fascinating and seductive building, if you like fascist architecture. The other building blighting the view is the new Ford Centre for Performing Arts, a lumpen factory for megamusicals that looks like a work boot with a grandiose entranceway at one end. The electronic marquee advertises the imminent opening of *Showboat*, fresh off its triumphant run at that other Ford Centre in that other world-class city, North York. This city is changing fast. Off in the distance, draped in cloud, are the beloved mountains.

To the production office, located on an industrial street in a spare suite of rooms in a chocolate factory. I meet the few production staffers who haven't been laid off. I am surprised and pleased to see so many women working on what is through and through a "guy picture." There's Anne Simonet, our production manager, Erin Smith, our coordinator, Wendy Ladret, our accountant, Patricia Baun, Christine's assistant. There's Rachel again, frantically scheduling a film that may or may not go into production, moving deftly between her notebook computer and a large wall calendar, breaking the foul-mouthed script down into shooting days structured around locations. (I note that all but three days of shooting will take place in Vancouver . . . so much for the big road circus we'd dreamt about.) There's Christine in the middle of another practicum in crisis management, chain-smoking as she juggles calls: this actor's agent demands to know the status of the film, that actor's agent demands more money, this other one demands perks we haven't got the budget for, one agent seems to be giving grief over uses of the actors' images in such potential products as Joe Dick dolls, Pipefitter dolls.

Meanwhile, B.C. Film can't tell Christine if they're investing or not because their guy who calls the shots is off in Italy. Someone from the press wants to know if the film is dead or alive. I can only imagine what it's been like for all these people, most of whom I don't even know, who have been working for weeks now to prepare this show.

Bruce tells me about his trip to L.A. The feelers are out and maybe we'll get a call. We have to assume we're moving forward, so we get down to discussing further small script changes. I find a corner and set to work marking up my script while Bruce is pulled this way and that by various people in various departments, and in a flash it's evening again.

Bruce, Hugh, Pyper, and I are joined for dinner by Danny Salerno, a pal of Bruce's from Toronto (and a coproducer of *Highway 61*) who is here to make a documentary film on the making of *Hard Core Logo*. I'd completely forgotten about this. When you think about it, the mind boggles. Salerno will be making a documentary about the production of a film about a documentary about a punk band's final tour. It's a hall of mirrors, a snake devouring its tail. There's even a guy working on a comic book derived from the script, not to mention a tribute album featuring several hot bands "covering" the HCL songs, to be released when the film comes out. On learning that I myself have a further contribution to this orgy of cross-exploitation in the form of this diary-book in progress, Salerno gets a bit down in the mouth. He didn't know about it, and he worries that what I'm writing will undermine the exclusivity of his own documentation of "the making of." I assure him that books and films rarely get in each others' way (unless you're adapting one into the other). I can't possibly tell the story in words that his camera is going to tell. And anyway, this book is but a tiny sliver of the big, fat, opportunistic, grabola pie that Michael Turner never realized he was baking when he first thought of Joe Dick.

18 October 1995

Production office. Things are really up in the air today. No one knows anything. Plug could be pulled any minute. Christine wanders around the office rigid, angry, anxious, on edge, snippy to talk to. The production staff tiptoe around on eggshells. Danny Salerno and his crew wander through the office capturing the tension on their cameras.

Meanwhile, Bruce and I write a discography for the band to kill time and try to keep our minds off the fact that our movie might be dead. We make up fake punk song titles, solicit them from production staffers, steal them from backlists of underground punk bands. Bruce's assistant Sandy faxes us a list of hilarious pornographic titles from Toronto. We mix in all of Michael Turner's titles from the book. Thus we compile an entire bogus recording history for the band.

```
1978 SON-OF-A-BITCH TO THE CORE (EP)
1. Son-of-a-Bitch to the Core
2. Sally Is a Popular Girl
3. Mobile Electric Chair
4. Fuck-Off America
5. Honky Night in Canada

1980 HARD KNOCK HIGH
1. Pigeon Park
2. Underwearwolf
3. Ten Buck Fuck
4. Lake Ontario Smells Like Shit
```

5. Bootlegger Song
6. She Said Kiss Me Where It Stinks (So I Drove Her to Squamish)
7. Bitch Slap
8. Hard Knock High
9. Welfare Case
10. Dressed Like Sally Ann

1981 US OUT OF NORTH AMERICA (EP)
1. Who the Hell Do You Think You Are?
2. Words and Music
3. Mt. Rushmore Strip Mine, Inc.
4. Undefended Border
5. Bring Out Yer Dead
6. Brown Spider

1983 THINK GLOBAL ACT STOOPID
1. Edmonton Block Heater
2. Let's Go Down to Hollywood (and Shoot Some People)
3. Drivin' with Chipper Johnson
4. Chicken's Gonna Die
5. Honest Injun
6. Blondes Have More Cum
7. The Only Chowder
8. Ready, Willing, and Anal
9. Vomitorium

1984 Ⓐ, EH?
1. Peace, Order, and Good Government
2. Life, Liberty, and Lotsa TV
3. Pit Bull Attack
4. Fucked in the Head
5. Misamerica
6. Can Nada Do
7. Herbie's Monster Burger

─────────────── let's go down to hollywood ───────────────

8. Vote Kill
9. Playing with a Full Dick
10. Let's Break Robert Out of Jail

1986 SOMETHING'S GONNA DIE TONIGHT (EP)
1. Something's Gonna Die Tonight
2. Something's Gonna Die Tonight (Dance Mix)
3. Something's Gonna Die Tonight (Shit Mix)
4. Something's Gonna Die Tonight (Meow Mix)

1988 ADULT COMICS
1. Fascist Gun in the West
2. Ode to Christa McAuliffe
3. Lyposuction
4. Snakes in My Head
5. There Is a God (and His Name Is Wilbur)
6. Blow Me Down
7. Built For Speedballs
8. Superantihero
9. Fist of Thorns
10. Sonic Reducer
11. Rocket Mensch

1989 ROCK 'n' ROLL IS FAT AND UGLY
1. The King in Diapers
2. Rock 'n' Roll Is Fat and Ugly
3. Bob Is Cool
4. Move or Die
5. European Supermodel
6. Twitch City
7. Gotterdammerung
8. Pacific Rim Job
9. Exquisite Corpse
10. Chunks
11. Beached Whale
12. Record Weasel

hard core roadshow

19 October 1995

I spend the day in a back room with the fridge, coffee maker, copier, making minor script revisions, hanging out. Waiting. Wondering if we're wasting our time here.

Christine and Karen have been playing a sort of three way ping pong with B.C. Film and Telefilm, sorting out budgetary details. These calls go on for hours, but finally, near the very end of the day, the call we've all been waiting for comes. B.C. Film has officially come through with THE MONEY!

Interestingly, there's none of that YEEHAAA! kind of feeling you might expect, but more of a thank-fucking-God-now-let's-get-on-with-it feeling. Relief. There's a brief celebration, then people hit the phones. We'll start shooting on the 25th or 26th now. Laid-off production staff will have to be rehired, the entire shoot rescheduled. We'll start rehearsals with the actors in a couple of days.

With the B.C. Film financing, there are rules about certain personnel. Miro is out, and a local cinematographer, Danny Nowak, is in. Nowak is in his mid-thirties, trained out here mainly on low budget features for video and Asia, as well as the usual music videos and commercials that fill the gaps in a busy DOP's schedule. He used to front a local punk band called The Spores. So he comes to us with a solid understanding of the life we're trying to portray. Better still, he loves shooting documentary-style, off the shoulder.

We also have to hire a local film editor as the post-production will have to be done in Vancouver now. For Bruce this means putting his Toronto-based life on hold for a while, perhaps several months, as he cuts the picture out here. At least he'll miss a Toronto winter. Bruce assesses our new timetable and says that we're going to aim for a Cannes premiere. This thing's rolling, and we're back to thinking and talking big.

20 October 1995

People from newspapers and radio stations call Bruce for interviews. All those who've somehow heard that the movie is dead (which seems to be everyone in town) have to be set straight. Over the phone Bruce repeatedly bills *Hard Core Logo* as "*Spinal Tap*'s mean little brother." Rock movie marketing made simple.

The script was sent to Miramax when things were looking bleak. All we were asking for was U.S. $350,000. When Bruce spoke to them in L.A., the Miramax people told him he should find some rich dentists to raise that kind of chicken feed, 'cause if Miramax were to enter the picture with production money, they'd be walking away with most of the profits. They were kind enough to say that if we can make this movie with other financing, we can later sell them the completed film and cut a much better deal. Today Miramax called back to say that they are in fact very, very interested in kicking in the money now. Bruce spends twenty minutes on the phone with the guy telling him that he's too late, we raised the rest of our financing from the Hell's Angels. The guy on the line freaks, says it's the wildest financing story he's ever heard, and he's going to run down the hall to tell Bob and Harvey (the Weinsteins, who run the company). Bruce hangs up and we all have a good laugh, the truth being so much less glamorous.

Other developments: now the money's in the bag, there are continuing problems confirming two of our lead actors. We might lose Callum and John due to scheduling conflicts. With our delay, we're cutting it close on other commitments for which the actors have signed contracts (nobody's signed anything with us yet). Then there's Bernie Coulson, whose agent seems to be doing some eleventh hour haggling over money. It gets to the point where a casting book is hauled out to see what other actors are available, should we need to replace our guys at the last minute.

*

Bruce's girlfriend, Heidi, is coming to visit for the weekend, and Hugh has offered to let me stay on the sofabed in his suite for a couple of days. I move my stuff in, get to know Hugh a little better.

Some things I've learned about Hugh: he's unfailingly loyal once you are his friend. He's very direct and honest. He has no fear of cutting through bullshit and voicing awkward truths. He likes gangs of guys, loves singing in a band. He loves being the leader. He takes no shit from most people, and yet he's willing to cede a lot of control over practical aspects of his life to his manager. He tends to ask his manager for permission to do certain things, like take money out of the bank. He phones his girlfriend and his songwriting partner just about every day. He's hard on hotel rooms. He smokes constantly but does not drink during production. He doesn't suffer fools. He tells me he has great respect for artists and writers, though thinks nothing of changing my dialogue. He is the same guy on-stage and off. He has integrity. He likes jokes. Shawn O'Hearn, our transportation captain, tells me the first words Hugh spoke to him: "So Shawn, I'm out last night and I meet this guy, right? Great guy, we're having a cool time, having some drinks. So afterward I go back to his place. And I'm fucking him, right? I mean really giving it to him. Then afterwards I'm zipping up, ready to split, right? And the guy wants to cuddle . . . What a fag, eh?"

21 October 1995

Callum is confirmed at last. But there's a lingering problem with Bernie, whose agent is still haggling for more money. Without a deal in place we begin rehearsals without him and I read the Pipefitter part during our first full read-through. The event is taped by Danny Salerno's camera for his documentary.

The reading goes well enough, and I'm especially impressed with Pyper, who has invented a stutter for John, which he exaggerates in the scenes after John has lost his lithium pills. Hugh is still a little shaky, but this could be that he's looking at lines on the page and "reading" instead of acting. Callum has had ten months to think about the nuances of Billy, and he is very good, though he tends to change his lines in order to sound cooler in places. Pyper gets in on this act and wants to change a couple of lines, based on the logic of what his character would and wouldn't say. No one leaps to the writer's defense. Christine catches my eye with a glint in hers, the glint of someone who knows a virgin screenwriter who's about to lose his cherry.

*

Later, a full scale production meeting with all the rehired personnel present. There are also several volunteers here, willing to work for nothing in various departments. Bruce addresses the troops, talks of how rough he expects the production to be, of turning limitations into virtues, of the struggle to land just the actors we wanted, of the need for the crew to work together to make the band seem as real as possible on screen. They are the faces, and we are the people who have to make the audience fall in love with them.

We want to make as much noise as possible, Bruce says. We may be small but we're still competing against big studio features. Bruce is calm, soft-spoken, genial. Not a table-thumping bully, not an evangelistic inspirer. Yet he has the ability to convey the specialness of the project at hand, do his job, and stand back and let everyone else do theirs.

23 October 1995, 4 a.m.

Bernie Coulson arrives from his home on Vancouver Island. Meet him in the hotel bar with Bruce, Hugh, Callum, and Pyper. Christine and his agent had been haggling all day, and Bernie was going stir-crazy over there, so he went out and played a round of golf stoned out of his mind. Heard the deal was sewn up when he got to the clubhouse, had some celebratory cocktails, went home, grabbed his bag, went to the airport, and, like, here he is.

Instantly Hugh, Callum, and Pyper start to figure out how Bernie's going to fit into this picture, where he's going to fall in the pecking order. As Bernie is already hammered, the others have him at a disadvantage, immediately spot his weaknesses, and move in without mercy. Within half an hour Bernie is the dumb drummer who can't get no respect. He instinctively knows this is to be his role in this group, whether the camera's rolling or not, and he takes to it like a duck to water.

Dinner with the four leads where like an anthropologist I watch them interact, looking for further last-minute script inspiration. Here I am at last, sitting with Hard Core Logo. The band created by Turner and built by Bruce. Our punk Monkees, Bruce says. During dinner, which is very loud thanks to Bernie, a couple approach and actually ask the guys if they are a band. Without missing a beat all four of them nod and reply "Hard Core Logo." A magical moment.

After dinner we head to the Town Pump to see DOA play, soak up some vintage Vancouver punk. We sit through a few songs, but I sense the Hard Cores want to be alone to get better acquainted. I wander off to watch the band through a couple of songs and when I return to the table the guys are gone.

Back at the hotel Hugh tells me he and the others had no interest in researching "their musical roots" by watching DOA.

First rehearsal.

23 October 1995, Evening

This afternoon "the band" runs through its first musical rehearsal in a basement studio at the chocolate factory, faking along to playback of the pre-recorded HCL songs. Bruce runs the tape machine, a rock 'n' roll Dr. Frankenstein in the lab, looking upon his creation, fiddling with some knobs to get it just right. The guys are ranged at their instruments, facing us as they would face a crowd. Callum's guitar coach, Ted Hall, stands in front of Callum playing along to the songs on his own guitar, demonstrating the correct fingerings, how to jerk the guitar, how to move with it. Seems to work: Callum does look like a guitarist. If I didn't know better I'd say he was a guitarist. Ditto for Pyper on bass, who stays in one spot and steps to a mike to belt out backup vocals. Bernie plays drums with total manic confidence, grinning, making crazy faces, ripping beer cans in half with his teeth, all without missing a beat. Hugh doesn't so much lip-synch or sing along as attack the mike. The band may be fake, but the small room jumps with real energy, sweat, and aggression. Bruce and I headbang along, exchange grins. It's working. The band Hard Core Logo are one step closer to reality.

24 October 1995

Evening. To the Malcolm Lowry Room to meet with Turner. The Malcolm Lowry Room, named in honor of the great drink-sodden author who once lived in Vancouver, is a barroom in an unremarkable little hotel on Hastings in Burnaby. For a few years Turner has organized events here (poetry, performances, etc.).

Danny Salerno brings his camera crew to tape the moment as Turner greets Bruce and me at the door. Extreme embarrassment when Bruce also wants to stage my giving Michael a copy of the screenplay in front of Danny's camera (even here a fake documentary moment). I'm actually a bit nervous, as Turner hasn't seen the script in any form. I joke that it's a

— let's go down to hollywood —

thorough corruption of his work and intentions. Turner plays along for the camera. I pull out the script with a flourish, write a dumb dedication on the blue laser-printed title page. Smiling, he flips through the script as the camera rolls, looking for his own writing rearranged into screenplay format. He turns page after page, intrigued, curious to see what has become of his characters and story. The smile fades as he starts turning pages furiously:

Hey, I don't see *any* of my writing in here, he says.

I shrug, give my now standard line about film being a hyperbolic medium, about writing the film that had to be made, etc.

Wait a minute, Turner says, here's something: "Fuck you."

Later we sit around a table. Bruce, Turner, Danny Nowak, Keith, me. *Roadkill*, rented for the occasion, plays on a big screen against the wall. Salerno's crew films the encounter. We talk about the long road to this moment, about rock 'n' roll mythology and the romance of the road, about the difference between the book Turner wrote and the script that Bruce is going to film. Turner is gracious, claims he trusts us to do right by the material and he understands that we can't simply film his book. He tells Danny Salerno's camera that film's like a country, while writing's like a small town. As the evening winds down he wishes us all broken legs. I ask him if he'll read the script. He says probably not.

4.

HERBIE'S MONSTER BURGER

25 October 1995, Day 1

Universe is unfolding as it should. The rain is falling in Vancouver and we are making *Hard Core Logo*. Bruce pokes his head through my bedroom door before leaving for the set at 6:30 this morning. I lie there groggy and hungover after last night's session. He thanks me for "being the one who got us here." Then he's out the door. True or not, his words leave me kind of choked up. They don't get me out of bed though. I slide back to sleep, figuring there won't be a first shot set up for at least a couple of hours.

Today's location: basement of the Town Pump in Gastown, walking distance from the hotel. I arrive late to find that I've missed the first scene. Things are moving faster than I thought.

The setting is the band's dressing room at the club in Regina; we're shooting stuff that takes place halfway into the story. It's a perfectly seedy room, much as I imagined it, with low ceilings, exposed joists, cobwebs, barrels of draft stacked in a corner, burn-pocked couches, the walls plastered with band graffiti (entirely done by our art department) including, exactly as indicated in the script, "HOW'S THE CAREER GOING?"

So, how *is* it going? Just fine. Finally, I'm on the set of a movie I've scripted, watching as words on a page are transmuted into actions on celluloid. I've worked for this moment for several years. The irony is, now I'm here there's nothing to do but stay the hell out of the way. I stake out a corner in the cramped room and watch the band's first big meltdown, which comes moments before their Regina show. The scene is electric, loaded with energy and emotional power. Bruce gets everything he needs in a few takes, including close-ups. The morning is quickly over. After lunch Bruce and I pause, look at the whole set, the dozens of cast and crew members, the trucks out back. He grins, says, We're doin' it, man!

*

Late in the evening, back at the hotel, more script work. Something about the sequence at Bucky's farm has been bothering me. We won't shoot it for another week, but I want to get it just right as soon as possible. The sequence feels wrong, it lacks the right emotional kick. Joe is metaphorically going to bury Bucky after the visit to the farm, but he needs a stronger reason to do this, especially if he is the one who used Bucky in the first place for the bogus benefit show.

Finally the idea hits: instead of being ignorant about Joe's bogus benefit concert in his name, Bucky knows about it all along. I rewrite Bucky's monologue so that he explains he left the music business because he was sick of being used by people. At the end of the visit to Bucky's farm, Bucky now pulls Joe aside and instead of wishing him well, he tells him he never wants to see him again, because Joe has now used him too. The ultimate betrayal in Bucky's eyes. Joe is skewered on the spot, abandoned by his idol. Meanwhile, Billy, who always hated Bucky, ends up walking away with the gift of Bucky's old Stratocaster guitar. It's a perfect equation: the cost to Joe of getting Billy back is his friendship with Bucky. Now when the band hit the stage in Saskatoon, Joe really has a reason to say that Bucky "died last night in New York City."

The conceptualizing of the film on paper, the construction of dramatic logic, of written lives, is far more abstract than

---------- herbie's monster burger ----------

I've admitted to myself. Even after a single day in production, I am seeing my own writing differently. I've begun seeing the "acted" lives of these characters, and this has me thinking about dozens of further changes and improvements we can make on the fly. I've read about lots of films where the biggest script changes take place in the middle of production. Only here can the physical opportunities be noted and seized.

26 October 1995, Day 2
A FAN'S NOTES:
This club is in one mighty frenzy. Sweating fans jam the floor in front of the stage, whooping and whistling, stomping in unison, screaming for an encore. The band rocked the house for like two hours and took us right to the edge. Are we done? No way, we want more more more and we want it now. Could get ugly if the band doesn't come back out soon. That's how it is with these rock mobs and their violent love.

Just as the bottles are about to fly a triumphant roar goes up from like six hundred voices and here come Joe, Billy, John, and Pipe for their encore. I scream and cheer with the rest until I'm hoarse. Then Joe, who always did know how to make a crowd eat out of his hand, steps to the mike and shouts "The West is the best!," which makes everyone nuts, and the band kick straight into "Sonic Reducer."

Man, I didn't dare hope they'd play it. Thought they'd pull some punk integrity thing and not play the hit. Like the time I saw Nirvana and they refused to do "Teen Spirit." But this is it baby, the big one, and the crowd at the band's feet is a magic carpet of throbbing, moshing, headbanging hardcore freaks going apeshit wild. Joe screams the words and holds the crowd like he was just touched by the finger of God. Billy

Tallent, the greatest thrash guitarist of all time, jerks supreme noise from his axe as the babes drool over him. Pipe beats the shit out of the skins while making these faces like a troll under a footbridge. Then there's steady-as-she-goes John (guy looks like Charlie Manson now he's grown his hair out) grinning his face off, thumping his bass, singing backup, excited as a kid to be back on the road with da boys. It's an explosive moment.

I see the rock press are out in force and you just know this one's going down in history. Calgary is the coolest place in the world to be right now. Joe screams "THINGS WILL BE DIFF-RENT THEN, THE SUN WILL RISE AGAIN, THEN AH'LL BE TEN FEET TALL, AND YOU'LL BE NUTHIN-AT-ALLLLL." What can I do but jack myself over a wall of backs and surf the crowd. Kill me now and I die a happy man, I am that blissed. Then some asshole yells "Cut!"

Music craps out. I'm dumped on the floor.

*

Town Pump, Vancouver, 9 a.m.
We're shooting performance footage from "Calgary" here this morning on the very same stage where we watched DOA play a few nights ago. This afternoon the band plays "Regina" once the stage is re-dressed. Hard Core Logo are lip-synching and "rocking" along to playback audio. A mere thirty or so extras jam the front of the stage. Danny Nowak shoots off the shoulder from behind them, walking back and forth on a riser, an assistant holding his hips to keep him from falling off. Someone pumps fog into the air to diffuse the light. Bruce spent an hour already priming the extras and coaching

herbie's monster burger

First gig to be filmed. Wagon wheel
on stage signifies Calgary, get it?

the band. Ted Hall took Callum through his lead guitar-guy moves earlier. All is fake. But for a hypnotic moment, between the first calls of "Action!" and "Cut!," when the band straps on the gear and the crowd starts screaming, we are at some club in Calgary and this is a night to remember.

Filmmaking, however, is the art of repetition, and as the morning wears on the illusion takes more work. We film the same thing over and over from different angles, stopping and starting, stopping and starting. By eleven, I'm sprawled in a chair doing a crossword puzzle, wondering what's for lunch.

In the afternoon we shoot another concert sequence, this time from "Regina," using the same stage, same extras, different styling, different backdrop, shot from a completely different vantage point from an overhead mezzanine. After this we rework the post-show interview scene from Calgary where Joe and Billy talk to a know-it-all young female rock journalist who is more interested in Billy's work with Jenifur than in Hard Core Logo. As originally scripted, Joe handles the interview like a politician or sports figure, giving prefabricated answers until the questions get too difficult to dodge and he snaps at the interviewer. Through it all he is in denial about Billy's lack of loyalty to him after all these years.

Bruce, Hugh, Callum, Nicole (the young actress playing the interviewer), and I knock ideas around for half an hour or so and I scribble out the scene on foolscap. When we rehearse the rewritten scene and film it, the denial and its attendant subtext are gone. The ugly energy of Joe's jealousy towards Billy is front and center, right on the surface. It hangs there and makes you cringe. Hugh is a powerhouse in the scene, playing Joe as an angry, unrepentant, unapologetic bastard. Perhaps because he's not a trained actor, Hugh is utterly unafraid of darkness or ugliness, of making a prick of his character. The honesty makes him completely sympathetic.

*

Late at night Hugh comes up to our suite and tells us he has a new idea for the end of the film, to do with his character. I'm thinking oh pleeese, go to bed and learn tomorrow's lines. But Hugh's just dying to get this off his chest, so we sit and listen. It takes about ten minutes for him to get to the end of his thought. Which leaves us kind of stunned. We know Hugh's onto something, something that gives the story a much stronger sense of closure than anything I've written. It's a shocking ending. It's huge. It changes everything.

Hugh sits down and we talk it through, getting more and more excited about it. Next thing we know it's three in the morning but we're too juiced to sleep. When Hugh leaves Bruce and I talk for another half hour, going over the script point by point, looking for ways to set up the new final scene. I stay up for a couple more hours, sketching in the changes. It's a ballsy ending, a huge risk, but we've shaken on it, there's no turning back. It's an ending we never would have considered without seeing two days of Hugh's performance. Now we know who Joe Dick really is, we know this will work, we know there is no other ending to this film. We'll shoot it on day 12.

27 October 1995, Day 3

Late start. Still inspired. Perky sunshine, a sweet day. Walk the few blocks to today's set, the Penthouse Club, a venerable boylesque dive (inasmuch as such places are ever "venerable"). There's even a brass pole on the stage and a runway jutting out into the room where the strippers strut. The Penthouse is standing in for a club in Saskatoon where the band play Bucky's song "Blue Tattoo" and where documentary filmmaker Bruce secretly films Joe and Billy making a pact to form a new band without John and Pipe.

Word of the new ending has leaked throughout the cast and crew. There's a sense of excitement and debate on the set. Some love it, some fear it. Midway through the day, Christine and Karen Powell arrive. They've heard the news and want to talk about it, they want to know what we think we're doing. I tell them.

Are we kidding?

Nope.

Have we thought through the implications?

More or less.

Worried looks are exchanged. Then all hell breaks loose. Christine thinks the new ending is simply insane. Karen wants to grab Bruce and set him straight right now. Christine pleads the artistic case for the present ending, coming up with a number of entirely valid reasons for not doing what we're talking about doing. I have to agree that there's nothing at all wrong with the ending as it is, except that it isn't as powerful as the new ending. (The "old" ending has Joe on the street after the final fight with Billy, handing the band's gig fee to a street busker, then dancing with an old man. Fade up text from Joe's classified ad for musicians to form a new band. The end.) The new ending is just better. It infuses all the earlier scenes with greater tension, meaning, subtext. The new ending will affect the timbre and calibre of the performances for the better.

They're not buying. Karen weighs in with objections rooted in contract law, saying that you can't go making substantial changes once you've signed off on the shooting script with distributors and other financiers. Once investors and distributors sign off, they expect the script to be transferred intact to the screen. Failure to deliver the contracted film is a breach of contract. Karen cites the case of *Mesmer*, starring Alan Rickman, which got caught up recently in the courts when the distributor sued the producers for delivering a different film from the one the distributor thought it had contracted. The film has not been released, and may never be, Karen says.* She goes on to warn me that this could be our fate if Bruce won't back down from his threat to shoot this new ending. Sounds ominous and I take these concerns seriously. When I pass all this on to Bruce later in the day, he shrugs and laughs, says he's already closed the vault on it. The

---

* *Mesmer* was released in Canada in early 1996, disappearing quickly from theaters.

new ending stays. And so the age-old struggle between art and commerce is to be played out here too.

*

Watching from the back of the club with Hugh's manager, Joe Bamford, as the band is filmed performing "Blue Tattoo." Between takes Bamford tells me that from the first moment he ever laid eyes on Hugh Dillon at a bar in Kingston some years ago, he knew he'd one day be standing on a movie set watching Hugh star in a film.

*

Some observations about our actors three days into shooting: Hugh's performance is far more powerful than I ever would have thought. The guy has an ego the size of King Kong, and it stands him in good stead here, since he's essentially playing himself. He is fearless, likes to challenge other actors and the camera. Joe Dick on paper is an angry guy. Hugh's Joe Dick is angrier still, uglier, but also perversely funny. Far funnier than I thought he'd be. Hugh plays it like he's got nothing to protect or lose because he *has* nothing to protect or lose. He's a rocker, not an actor. He's going on tour with Headstones as soon as this movie is finished. He's not worried about future acting jobs. He doesn't need to worry about being typecast as an asshole.

Callum Rennie is constantly looking for ways to boil his role down to a single essence, to simplify, to say less while being more. He may have been very candid about certain things when I first got to know him last May, but with the film in production I find him impenetrable (not that I have any interest in penetrating him). Billy has Callum's own remoteness, that sense of being preoccupied with the future, of constantly strategizing, calculating, looking ahead to a bigtime that might well await if only the right moves are made now. The single essence Callum seeks for Billy is, I think, the single essence he is seeking for himself, where person and persona commingle. It's an apprenticeship in The James Dean Way and it's fascinating to watch, on and off the set. Callum's two primary cool actor gestures: he points at people with his ring finger and this signifies many unspoken things (hello, good-bye, you're cool, I'm cool, fuck you, touché), he runs his hand through his hair, his head tilted down, when he looks harried or put-upon. It's the simplicity of his signifiers that makes him so effective as a screen actor.

John Pyper-Ferguson finds unexpected ways to work with the text exactly as he finds it written. He alone is actually delivering his scripted lines pretty well word for word, yet he is the one full of the biggest surprises in performance. His John Oxenberger is heartbreakingly vulnerable. The disintegration of John's personality mirrors the disintegration of the band, and the stuff I've seen him do from the middle of the story has to be the most difficult of all, because this is where John is on the cusp, just beginning the crackup. Pyper has the chops to go within seconds from a child's laugh to a schizophrenic's frustrated tears to a confused funk. It's a quiet and superbly modulated performance. He is the actor's actor of the bunch.

Bernie Coulson is a completely different kind of actor. Like Hugh, he never exactly nails his lines as written, and this forces him to improvise. He's a loose cannon, a card, a cut-up, one of those people who seems to live completely in the moment. Which is a form of genius that I admire. Bernie has

―――― herbie's monster burger ――――

Wall-to-wall thesps.

the ability to create high comedy out of nothing, a talent for framing the most apt images in just a few tossed-off words. Some of the stuff that comes out of his mouth is so brilliantly weird you don't want to rein him in too much for fear you might lose a Bernie-ism that's better than anything in the script.

28 October 1995, Day 4

We shoot the Edmonton band house stuff, and the Regina motel. Everything is going very smoothly on the set. We are "getting our days" as they say, shooting pretty well everything we scheduled, slightly more than five script pages per day. At our budget level (under $1.5 million), we can't afford overtime for the crew, so we're limited to twelve-hour shifts. Which means somebody's doing something right to keep this thing moving so smoothly and quickly.

––––––––––––––– hard core roadshow –––––––––––––––

On most film sets you usually find someone barking orders and directing traffic. We don't exactly have anyone doing that around here. What we do have is Rachel Leiterman, our first assistant director. Her professional vocabulary is the same as most first ADs': "Okay, here we go." "Quiet for rehearsal, please." "Watch your backs." "Roll sound." "Ready?" "First positions, everybody." "Let's go again." "Let's move on." Unlike many first ADs I ran across in my brief, sad career as a production assistant in the late 80s, she never raises her voice, she's unfailingly nice, cheerful, polite. Yet she commands respect. The crew snaps to it when she speaks. Everything motors along, setup after setup. No delays, no disasters.

It also helps that Bruce works unflappably. He never rages at crew or actors, never raises his voice. It's not like he has to pull any strange tricks or mind games on these actors to sharpen them up or prepare them for scenes. It looks from the outside as if he's quietly having a good time. He doesn't panic. He doesn't sweat a lot of the details (though sometimes I wish he would, seeing as I scripted most of them). Even though we're sharing a hotel suite and talk extensively every night about potential script improvements, how to have the actors play certain scenes, how well things are going so far, I really don't know what goes through Bruce's mind when he's directing, whether he feels like he's completely in control, like he knows exactly what he's doing every minute. What I do know is that he makes it look easy.

*

In the evening dailies are screened at Comet Post, where the film's editor, Reg Harkema, is a partner. Reg nightly takes us through the previous day's work on video monitors (the film is transferred to video daily). We watch, drinking the beer

---------- herbie's monster burger ----------

that is always in his office refrigerator. The people you find at dailies: director, cinematographer, producers, editor, production designer, sound recordist, writer (where he/she hasn't been barred from the production altogether). The actors do not come. Bruce doesn't want them getting self-conscious about their performances or chins or whatever.

The raw takes are thrilling so far, crackling with heat, humor, and pathos. From the first night it's been apparent that we're making a really good film. The camera loves Callum. Bernie is vivid and funny. Pyper's fractured performance is pitched perfectly for the camera. Hugh is simply scorching. He dominates. What excites me most is that several of us sit and watch, and it doesn't feel so much like work as entertainment.

*

Evening. Out with Christine, Karen, and Brian Dennis, who has just arrived from Toronto. Brian has been informed of the new ending, and he adds his voice to Christine and Karen's opposition, but for different reasons. Like Christine he fears the new ending is illogical, but more than this he is sure it will be damaging for box office. We discuss the issue late into the evening, and everyone wants me to talk to Bruce and try to get him to consider shooting an alternate ending along with the new one to give us a fallback position should we need one. Sounds like a reasonable request to me. Back at the hotel I relay the suggestion to Bruce. He says one word: Milquetoast.

29 October 1995, Day 5

Headline in the *Georgia Straight* says it all:
   "BAND REUNITES TO PLAY FIRST GIG"

──────────── hard core roadshow ────────────

Art Bergmann on location at the Commodore Ballroom.

*

The Commodore Ballroom is on Granville Street above some shops. Built in the 30s or 40s. Hosted everything that came down the pike over the years: big bands, nightclub floorshows, jazz combos, blues outfits, rock 'n' roll bands, reunions, corporate Christmas parties, benefits, hoedowns, costume balls, Empress balls, charity balls, bingo/casino nights, punk, thrash, and grunge, hip-hop, house, acid jazz, all of it. Holds about a thousand people. This is where we shoot today. And tonight, this is where Hard Core Logo will "reunite" to benefit Bucky Haight and "No More Guns."

Partial list of bands I saw at the Commodore in the early 80s when I still lived out here: Ramones about three times, Iggy about three times, XTC, Magazine, Pere Ubu, Dead Boys (they did "Sonic Reducer"), Specials, Gun Club, Gang of Four, the Cramps, Undertones, John Cale, the Beat, Stranglers, U2, New Order, James Brown, Psychedelic Furs, X, Black

Flag, Dead Kennedys, Chris Spedding, the Cure, David Johanson, Bootsy Collins, Violent Femmes, Burning Spear, REM, Love and Rockets, Rank and File. Partial list of the local bands, opening for these people: K-Tels/Young Canadians, Modernettes, Pointed Sticks, DOA, UJ3RK5, Braineaters, 54–40.

*

If you're ever making a film that has a rock concert setting and you need about a thousand extras to show up and be part of the crowd, do what this production has done and promote the thing as a real event and make people pay to be in the film. On the bill are: DOA, Art Bergmann, the Modernettes, Flash Bastard, Lick the Pole, and Miss Adrian (a drag act). And of course, Hard Core Logo.

During the day Bruce and the actors film scenes here and there in the Commodore. The large post-concert party scene contains dozens of extras, all recruited from the alternative music scene, past and present. Bit of a circus atmosphere, the musicians, doing their best to be cool, still subtly jockey for position to get into shots. Some of these people I knew fairly well, some I vaguely remember. I talk to old acquaintances between takes and many of them wonder what my connection is to this film. Someone introduces me to Buck Cherry of the Modernettes, a musician I admired but never really knew, and tells him that I wrote the screenplay. Buck looks at me a touch witheringly and says, You mean the adaptation. Like he's furnishing a much needed correction to some uppity claim I might be making to original authorship.

Adapted or original, a screenplay is still a screenplay. In any case, I make no claim to original authorship here, whatever my prior feelings about "moving beyond" the book in the name of drama. All my work is an extrapolation from, or reaction to, a superb book which I've been very proud to be associated with.

There's something more, though. I wonder if this guy means not so much adaptation as misrepresentation. People in this scene are very possessive about the movie. For months Keith Porteous has kept me apprised of some of the local rumors people have started about their involvement with the film, rumours rooted in fantasy and wishful thinking. Some people think that any movie set in the local music scene must be their story. They are suspicious of the Toronto-based filmmakers, and seem convinced that we are going to get it all wrong. Personally, I thought the Vancouver punk scene was electrifying in the late 70s/early 80s, but if we loaded the script with all the exactly "right" local details, the movie would be a snore. In the end, the script represents only that which is useful to the telling of a powerful story.

*

A different feeling of punk possessiveness outdoors, when we shoot scenes of crowds gathering in front of the Commodore on the Granville Mall. I hear a couple of young panhandling street punks complain about this "pseudopunk" movie "exploiting" them, their way of life, the things they stand for. These ones haven't quite got it right either. If there's anything the film is exploiting, it is the struggle of people who sing for their supper, not people who beg for it.

*

In the evening the paying audience files into the Commodore and the place fills up. I wonder if any of these people think their hard-earned cash is actually going to benefit some guy

herbie's monster burger

named Bucky Haight, or some anti-gun lobby called No More Guns. The concert begins, and we film it throughout the night with two handheld cameras. Danny Nowak is on-stage for some of it, and backstage to shoot scenes with the actors as they wait for their turn to go on. There's a sense of excitement building backstage as Hard Core time approaches. Just before Lick the Pole hit the stage, Bruce tells me to grab my script and follow him.

We go with Hugh, Callum, Bernie, and Pyper to the trailer behind the Commodore for a quick rehearsal of the stage stuff. Hugh has a problem with his intro speech to the crowd. The scripted lines are much as they were in the book, but Hugh doesn't want to say them. He wants to be a little rougher on the crowd. No problem, I'll just be happy if he doesn't hork greenies on them. We spend twenty minutes jamming out a new intro speech, which I print with magic marker on the back of a poster and later tape to Hugh's playback monitor on stage. With the words out of the way, the guys do an air guitar rehearsal as the boombox blasts through "Who The Hell Do You Think You Are?" and "Sonic Reducer." The adrenaline is pumping. They're ready.

Back inside the Commodore, the actress playing Laura Cromartie takes the stage and welcomes "Vancouver's favorite bad boys of punk." I head out onto the floor to watch Hard Core Logo's reunion performance. The guys take the stage to what is in fact half-hearted cheering from the crowd. Nobody from the crew has come onto the stage to prompt the crowd to scream their guts out for the movie. Except for the keeners right up front, most people stand with their arms folded, waiting to be impressed.

Moment of truth arrives when Hugh grabs the mike. Grins at the camera. Looks down briefly to check his lines taped to the playback monitor, then nails them perfectly, finishing up the speech with his own addition: "You don't know shit from good chocolate, babies!" The music kicks in, loud. The guys are "playing" again, but this time on a real stage for a paying audience. Hugh kisses Callum on the cheek. Then John. Then he starts in at the mike, sings along to his vocals. Callum keeps up his end, moving like a real guitarist but concealing his fretwork from prying eyes. Bernie plays along as usual, looking like a maniac at the kit, doing this Gene Simmons tongue-flicking thing. The spit flies from all four mouths.

For a moment it feels like the old days. I'm standing on the sprung dancefloor in the middle of the crowd, bouncing up and down, can of beer in my hand. Must have done this fifty times here. The band look real enough and sound real enough. Though most people in the crowd are aware that this is a movie, one disappointed rock fan shoves his way back past me with a know-it-all look, complaining, "These guys aren't even playing." Like, duh.

After the two songs, our actors go offstage and the process is repeated. By the second run-through the crowd in front of the stage is noticeably thinner. Bruce says it's no big deal, we'll just cut DOA's more frenzied crowd shots into the HCL performance footage. We'll boost crowd noise on the soundtrack. In the cutting room Reg will reconstruct a far more fabulous reality than there ever was here.

30 October 1995, Day 6

Just the facts today. Midmorning. Arrive on set in an industrial area near the production office to find the following scene in progress: the four members of HCL are dressed as the Beatles from *A Hard Day's Night,* and they are running away from a screaming mob of teenaged girls in Catholic schoolgirl uniforms — white blouses, sweaters, tartan skirts, kneesocks, sensible shoes. Two of the girls trip and fall to the pavement. One breaks a tooth, the other sprains something and winds up with scrapes. Good thing we're insured.

Bigger than Jesus.

Later, during lunch, Danny Salerno interviews some of the girls, who look to be fifteen or sixteen, for his documentary. One saucy little minx, a sort of bad girl ring leader, is in — as Shakespeare would put it — "a holiday mood." Smelling a Moment, Salerno draws her out and within seconds she faces his camera leading three of her cherubic friends through a chant which goes something like, "Fuck me fast, fuck me slow, fuck me high, fuck me low, fuck me left, fuck me right, fuck me hard all through the night . . ." Their earnest middle-aged chaperone from the school misses this, but Salerno interviews her later and she tells him how wonderful it is for these young girls to get out of the classroom and appear in a movie, how important it is for them to broaden their horizons, spread their wings, and have novel experiences.

*

In the afternoon we shoot inside a warehouse crammed with huge circus props and parade floats. Danny Salerno interviews me for his documentary, as he does most days. As the writer I'm more available to him than others who have actual work to do on the set. Danny often asks for my thoughts on the production. Are things as I'd envisioned them when I was writing the script? Some things are, some aren't. Am I disappointed by the things that aren't as I'd imagined they'd be? Sometimes, but just as often not. Sometimes the unexpected is better than anything I could have imagined. How about today, Danny asks, is this basically what I'd imagined when I wrote the sequence?

I look around. The warehouse has a menacing carnival air, with fat elephants, sinister giant clowns, spears, cages, parade float paraphernalia, in rows and piles throughout. A banquet table is set with white linen and china, and a big serving pot loaded with disgusting meat in a red sauce that oozes all over the place. This is the human flesh that our obese rock stars are going to be gorging themselves on during the "Rock 'n' Roll Is Fat and Ugly" music video sequence that opens the film. A woman of exceedingly tiny stature (a bit under three feet) stands atop the banquet table in a chef's hat, serving up the human flesh to two heavyweight camp versions of Elvis and Madonna. Nearby is a large cannibal pot over a roaring flame, painted with the word FANZ. Inside it sit two buck

herbie's monster burger

"Rock 'n' Roll Is Fat and Ugly"

naked young actresses willing, I guess, to do anything for a career break.

I tell Danny I can't believe someone didn't rip these pages out of the script months ago. I can't believe we're doing this at all.

*

Turns out I know our Elvis. He is Sid Morozoff, an old acquaintance, who has slipped into the world of Elvis impersonation in years past. A noble calling. What makes Sid stand out from the rest: he does a very fay late-period Elvis-in-Vegas shtick with a pair of haute queen sidekicks, who also appear in the tableau. Turns out I know this buxom Madonna too, as she is played by the very same Miss Adrian who performed as Marilyn at the Commodore last night.

We film the stars eating the flesh, tugging toes off feet with their teeth and so on. We film the girls screaming in the pot over the fire. Then we film the four members of HCL, still got up as the Beatles, as they escape from the school girls and take refuge inside the weird warehouse, only to discover the fans being eaten by the stars. Then things get interesting, cinematically speaking. The guys try to stop the cannibals, but Madonna is one step ahead of them and she pulls a canvas sheet off of a mounted machine gun and opens fire at the guys, spraying them with bullets.

*

We have a pyrotechnician on the crew named Scotty, who is the nicest, gentlest, and most genial guy you could ever imagine, for someone who dedicates his life to blowing shit up. Scotty takes a couple of hours to set squibs all over the actors and explain the dos and don'ts of squib scenes. Squibs are little charges that are concealed under the clothes and attached to little packs of fake blood. They are connected to wires which run down under the clothing and come out the bottom of the pant leg. The wires run across the floor to a detonator, which Scotty controls with a practiced hand. For each switch he throws, a squib explodes with a *pop* as from a capgun. The force is often strong enough to blow a hole in the clothing for the blood to come shooting out. The effect is, naturally, of a bullet ripping into a human body. Peckinpah made slow-motion squib effects his trademark.

*

Hugh, Callum, and Bernie stand together, the camera tight on them. They are facing the spot where Madonna will be wielding her machine gun. Bruce calls "Action!," and

herbie's monster burger

suddenly there are loud popping noises, and the guys have blood gushing out of them, and they all make like Al Pacino at the end of *Scarface*, doing a body-jerking St. Vitus' dance as the bullets cut into them mercilessly. They end up quivering on the floor, soaked in gore. That's a print, a one-take deal. Then we do Pyper, who is going to do his own death scene in a version of John Woo slow motion. Which is pretty funny, when the blood starts gushing from him and he slowly teases out this balletic death-of-a-swan swoon to the floor.

All this is shot MOS (no sound). Adding a further surreal touch to the day's work is the sound coming from a radio playing across the studio. Nonstop CBC news coverage of the Quebec referendum. Throughout the early evening we hear of a neck-and-neck race between Yes and No. Tensions are running high across the country. The fate of the nation hangs in the balance and we are busy filming a picnic of cannibal queens. Finally, the No side wins by less than one percent, a virtual split that sees the status quo maintained. Great relief as Quebecers prove themselves psychologically Canadian after all, unable to make up their minds about what they really want.

Satisfied that the country will just barely remain whole, we kill the radio and get back to the important business at hand, filming our drag queen Madonna as she grits her teeth and mows down Hard Core Logo with her machine gun.

*

Dailies are screened after shooting ends. Stuff from the Commodore and from the previous day. Everything is looking great on film. Every night that we gather to see the footage, we can see that the magic is being sustained day by day. It lives and breathes, this film. It throbs with raunchy energy.

Tonight Christine wants to stay afterwards and have a little meeting with Bruce and me about the new ending. She's tried a number of approaches to get Bruce to reconsider, but Bruce has been too busy to sit down and go through the whole issue point by point. So we sit down in the boardroom. Christine politely starts outlining her objections once more. But Bruce is tired and he's just had a big long-distance argument with his girlfriend in Toronto, and he cuts Christine off and says, "I don't fucking care, we're doing it and that's that." Long tense ugly silence. Christine sits there with her jaw set like cement. Bruce sits there with a red-faced grin, the look of Mr. Nice Guy as he transforms into Mr. Nice Guy-No-More. I sit there making mental notes on how best to write this moment up.

*

Writer's POV: So okay, it's awkward, being at loggerheads with our producers. I'm on Bruce's side here and want to go with the new ending. It's not a rational choice but an intuitive one. It just feels like the right way to go. But obviously our producers have legitimate concerns here. What if we film the new ending and incur the wrath of investors and distributor, who think they've sunk their money into a different film? What if they sue us? What if the ending comes off looking implausible or forced or stupid anyway? What if Everest refuses to release the film?

Brian, Christine, and Karen are the ones familiar with our investor contracts, they know what all the clauses and subclauses state about our warranties to deliver the film they have sunk money into based on the script. Can't blame them for being nervous. Still, this is a creative process and things can change. Is Bruce really being "irresponsible" here, as our producers have called him? Or is he seizing an opportunity to improve the film? Anyway, screenplays are never fixed in place until they are actually filmed. Another rationalization: business types have no problem demanding changes that suit them, so they should be prepared to accept inspired changes from the creative end.

*

Back to the boardroom. We keep sitting there and sitting there with Bruce and Christine staring stonily ahead, not looking at each other. Eventually Christine lurches to her feet and offers us a ride back to the hotel. Obviously this would be a good time to walk, but I'm curious to see what'll happen in the car. We walk to the car without speaking. We get in. She starts it. Then she drives us back to the hotel in ear-splitting silence. I get out and Bruce and Christine remain in the car for a long, long time.

31 October 1995

Day off. Bereft of clean clothes, I buy more to avoid doing laundry. In the afternoon more dailies are screened, with footage from earlier in the week that we haven't seen yet. Other than a few angry twitches when I hear the actors changing some of my favorite lines, I relax and marvel at the strong emotional truth of the performances.

*

This evening MuchMusic airs a special on *HCL* and the "Rock Against Guns" night at the Commodore. On TV Hugh takes the opportunity to relentlessly promote Headstones. Bernie is also in top form, wearing a kilt and long-nosed mask for the cameras. He asks TV host Terry David Mulligan (who has a small role in *HCL* as a booking agent) if he wants to see what he's got on under the kilt. Terry says, Sure. Bernie lifts his kilt for the camera. A surprisingly large blackout spot appears on the screen between his legs.

Terry goes on to interview a number of the old guard of Vancouver punk from the Commodore set, including Art Bergmann (bemused by the whole thing), Joey Shithead of DOA (reminding viewers about who really wrote the book on Canadian punk), and Buck Cherry of the Modernettes. Terry asks Buck how he feels about all the attention the punk revival is getting in the media. Buck just stares at him and says, Where were you assholes fifteen years ago?

Mulligan as music biz weasel Mulligan.

1 November 1995, Day 7

The crew shoots at various street locations around downtown this morning. Catch up with them at midday, at an alley around 4th and Main, where we shoot Pipe on the front porch (his

Vancouver home) talking to the camera with his girlfriend, and later John, burning his diary off the back porch (Edmonton), tying up the diary scene shot a few days ago. Single exterior locations are doubling for entirely different cities.

John's performance as he burns the diary for the camera is one of those ones where directors put their arms around the actor afterward and both cry their eyes out. This is perhaps the most heartfelt and sad moment of the film. The only thing keeping John grounded in reality goes up in flames. He delivers the "words come and go, but pictures never die" line with real tears in his eyes and I get all choked up. A writer's moment, no question.

2 November 1995, Day 8

On Homer, more or less across the street from Comet Post near what they now call Yaletown sits a nightclub called The Starfish Room. Which used to be Club Soda. Which used to be The Quadra. Which was a dyke bar. A bar I drank at precisely twice, back in the early 80s. The straight hipster crowd was starting to infiltrate the place, it being cool and dangerous to hang with stone butch dagger dykes. This probably led to the regular clientele deserting, and the club's transformation into the safe-for-the-straight-crowd Club Soda (the name says it all). First time I drank at The Quadra was a riot. Strange, wondrous new world o' women who run with other women. The second time I drank there, I made inadvertent eye contact with a demure slip of a girl in a white dress.

Thought nothing of it.

Within seconds, a hulking amazon lumberjack lezzie swaggered over, took off her fat belt, and threatened to pound the piss out of me with her Harley buckle for "making goo-goo eyes" at her "wife." Glanced over at the girl in the white dress. Halfway proud to see the hubby starting up another brawl over her.

A skill I've always had is for vividly anticipating outcomes. This is what I saw in a flash: me, with two black eyes and a reverse imprint of the Harley-Davidson logo across my forehead, and everyone knowing that I was worked over by a possessive lesbian. I made a gracious (not to say cowardly) exit, and haven't been back until now.

*

So here we are, The Starfish Room. The old Quadra much on my mind this morning. Until Mom shows up. She'd been asking when she could come visit the set, when would be the best time, what would be the best location? Well I could put her off no longer and suggested she drop down here for a couple of hours this morning, as today we'll be shooting the Edmonton club sequence, the last performance, where Joe has learned of his betrayal by Billy and attacks him on the stage. Rock 'n' roll performance, big fight, John's spoken-word freakout, the works. Lots of excitement. I'm happy to have Mom here, though in an adolescent way, a bit worried I'll get razzed for it. Worse, I fear that Danny Salerno will interview her and tape stories about me that only a mother should know.

Mom takes a seat with a good view near the back of the club and hangs there. All day long. Taking it all in. We shoot mostly ear-splitting nonstop performance footage, with a crowd of freaks for fans recruited off the streets by our resourceful extras casting team. I notice one punky kid in the crowd, back of his T-shirt says, ". . . but I never fucked your daughter."

herbie's monster burger

Pyper comes out of a back room for rehearsal on stage, smeared from head to toe in white makeup, wearing naught but a jockstrap and a ladies' white ski jacket with furry trim. For he is John Oxenberger, a lad insane.

With every song performed for the camera (there are about five), the band becomes more and more intense. John gets snakier. Joe angrier. Billy glibber. Pipe glummer. The energy, all this nasty, ugly, pent-up rage, starts to permeate the room for real.

Nonetheless, Mom's really enjoying the whole process. During breaks she meets this Bruce fellow she's heard so much about and finds him to be very sweet for a guy who looks like a biker. Christine welcomes her to the set. Mom thinks her gracious. Bernie comes up and gives her a big hug, says "Hi, Mommmmm." He's cute and funny, she says. Hugh walks by, pauses, says "Don't tell me . . . Noel's mom, right? It's the eyes." Later, watching Hugh strut around on stage between takes, she says, "He certainly doesn't have a self-esteem problem, does he?"

She meets Joe and John, the sound guys, who crack her up with songs they make up as they work. Danny Nowak says hi. So does Rachel. She meets Dean Paras, the actor playing a college radio interviewer. People bring her herbal tea from the craft service table. Everyone tells her what a Talent her son is (as they have been paid to do). Everyone thinks my mom's just great. My mom thinks the whole thing is just so neat. Finally, a movie scripted by her boy.

"I'm so proud of you," she whispers as I gaze at the punky kid spotted earlier. The front half of his T-shirt reads, "I may have fucked your son."

*

I'm off pretending to have something to do when Danny Salerno, the evil bastard, corners Mom at last with his camera crew and starts interviewing her. Spot them from across the room and feel the panic welling within. I drift close enough to hear Danny saying, "So when Noel was a boy . . ." Danny has her on camera during shooting breaks for a total of what seems like six hours. I can't bear this and stay as far away as possible. Later I ask her what she told him. Nothing to be ashamed of, she says. I'll have to take her word for it.

*

Danny Salerno is really on his game today. Leaving no stone unturned in his quest for novel angles in "The Making of *Hard Core Logo*," he starts interviewing these two big chunky shaved-headed punks who've turned up as crowd extras for three days of production.

What Salerno wants to know of these fellows is what they do when they're not working on films. What they do is this: drive around in a van scooping up corpses and body parts from road accidents and other death sites. One of their dads owns the business, as a sort of a subcontractor to the city coroner. It's a steady job, mainly nights. Good coin, they can't complain. Sometimes they'll stop at a party and leave body parts in the back of the van. Whatever. There's no rush getting the stiffs where they're going. You have to picture how blasé these guys are.

They tell a classic slacker suicide story about two rotting corpses they scooped up a while back. Two young French-Canadian guys had driven their van all the way across the country on a pilgrimage to the site of Kurt Cobain's grave in Seattle, where they planned to blow their brains out in homage to their hero. However, when they got to Vancouver,

herbie's monster burger

they were running out of money, started thinking about potential hassles at the border, the high cost of procuring a gun Stateside, the mandatory seven-day wait for a permit (no fun when you're broke and can't eat). In the end driving the extra three hours down to Seattle to kill themselves just seemed like too big a hassle, so instead they parked themselves in someone's garage in Vancouver, locked the door, turned on the engine, and asphyxiated themselves, leaving a ho-hum note explaining all. Man, are these kids today apathetic or what?

*

Eight p.m. Last thing we shoot is what will be the film's final interior scene. The band finishes "Something's Gonna Die" and Joe attacks Billy. John raves my doggerel into the mike until the fight ends, repeating the words, "In the end it's love," until Pipe gently takes the mike away and bellows, "Thank you Edmonton! Good Night!" The scene gets covered from a few different vantage points. Then, for one final shot, as the camera tracks with Billy who is walking out on Joe forever, Danny Nowak wants everyone he can get into the shot for background. So Mom and I stand at the back to help bulk out the crowd. The larger of the cadaver-scraping punks stands next to us, and Mom ends up talking to him, and she just can't resist letting it slip that her son, me (she points), wrote the screenplay to this movie. Guy looks confused. "Screenplay? I thought this was a documentary."

3 November 1995, Day 9

Halfway there already! We are in Surrey or Delta or somewhere in the middle of the wide, flat Fraser Valley, near the

U.S. border, at a small hog farm, for the filming of scenes at Bucky's Saskatchewan farm. Most of the production vehicles are parked on a road about a hundred yards from the set. Very nippy out here this morning and I walk to the set with a Kinky Friedman line in my head: it's colder than blue eyes that don't love you any more. There's a small two-track bridge that crosses over a wide ditch. First thing you see: a pig-pen with a pair of fat porkers inside. Next thing: a scarecrow wearing a blue tuxedo with a guitar strapped on, pumpkin for a head, as scripted. Then there's the gothic clapboard farmhouse, surrounded by a clutch of trees, a few old cars, wild uncut grass. A dilapidated verandah runs around three sides of the house. Only thing missing is Norman Bates. This is home for the next two days.

*

For the first time we use the band's van in a shot. It is a square box, the kind used by bakeries and courier companies. The interior is a horrific, dingy mess, the walls covered with road graffiti from innumerable bands who have actually used this van on tours. Two seats up front, benches along walls in back. Loads of space to maneuver in. On the outside our art department has stenciled a goat's head onto the back, along with the words, "Meats and Dairy." We've already taken to calling it "the goat van." It's perfect.

*

We shoot the guys stepping from the goat van as they arrive at the house; Bucky walking out onto the porch on two perfectly good legs; Bucky greeting the guys as they come up the steps to his house. Then scenes inside the house, where Bucky tells his sordid tales about life in the rock 'n' roll

herbie's monster burger

On set in Bucky's kitchen.

passing lane. Hugh, Callum, Bernie, and Pyper are hugely impressed with Julian Richings, who completely nails his enormous part, word for word, every single take.

We shoot a scene where Joe comes out of the house to talk to director Bruce, who is now aware of the fact that the benefit and tour are scams. As Bruce is actually in the scene, he risks creating a monster by allowing me to call "action" and "cut" through five takes.

Lunch time comes and goes. When it is time to resume filming, we notice that Bernie Coulson is missing. Hugh finds him upstairs, fast asleep in a bed. He rips the covers back to discover Bernie curled up clutching a teddy bear. Hugh, who is ruthless in these matters, calls him "Snuggles" for the rest of the day.

*

Mid-afternoon. Sitting inside the house listening to two crew members grousing. One guy is complaining that he no longer has a life of his own, hasn't done laundry in months, hasn't had a meal at home, hasn't seen his girlfriend, hates being trapped out here, working on someone else's film when he'd rather be doing one of his own.

A woman on the crew says that at least the guy has a relationship. The topic shifts to sex and I learn some interesting things about lives spent as members of film crews. Unattached production crew people work such long hours that most of their relationships are with fellow crew members. The accidents of hiring and casting throw people together intensely for a few weeks or months, then pull them apart again. Meaningless sex with coworkers is better than no sex at all, right? Affairs end when productions end and people move on to different crews. Maybe you'll never see the person you had an affair with again. But for the brief time you are on a production crew, the people around you become confidantes, family, lovers, gangmembers. You spend more time with them than you do with anyone else. So many people working in film production have seen relationships split up because they simply don't have time to spend with spouses or families. Production schedules are harrowing. Often six-day weeks, fourteen or sixteen-hour days. Leaving enough personal time for people to go home, sleep, shower, return to work. It's a hard life.

*

Bruce has spoken of the production period as a campaign, as if it's part of a war. For me it's a holiday. From writing, from planning, from hustling. From my civilian life. Battles have their own momentum and energy, their own pace and force. Some people find them addictive and magical. Filming is a "war measures" period that imposes its own conditions. Normal rules no longer apply. You simply obey the film's demands. You react. You seize opportunities as they arise. Intellectual labor is not required. Being here is enough. All these people show up on the set every day, and every day magic happens in the heat of battle. Our common goal gives us uncommon energy. Day after day I look around and think I never want this to end, never want to go home or return to the writing life. Feel like the soldier who precedes Willard upriver in *Apocalypse Now*, the one who went after Kurtz only to be seduced by the thrill of unending battle. The one who sends his wife the note that reads, "SELL THE HOUSE, SELL THE KIDS, I'M NEVER COMING BACK!"

3 November 1995, Evening

Return to the hotel to find a message from Siobhan. I call home. There's a complication with her pregnancy. An amnio test has revealed a higher than normal chance that our baby will have Down's Syndrome. Another test culture has been taken to verify the initial indication, but the results won't be known for two weeks.

That's it. Fuck it, I'm out of here, I'm going home. There's nothing I can do about the test, but I can be with Siobhan until the results come. Siobhan tells me to hang on. Aren't I in the middle of something important? Sure, but this is more important. Siobhan tries to put me at ease somewhat, explaining that the "higher than normal" chance of Down's is still a longshot. And anyway, she'll be swamped with work of her own through the next few weeks. My presence would be a comfort, but won't change anything. We talk it through and agree that I'll stay put for the time being.

Later I reflect, in a sort of callous writerly way, on the truism that complications like this exist in life and in narrative precisely to school the heart in what it most wants, to heighten the value of the heart's desire. I vow to use this sharp powerful feeling, this notion, in my future work. And then I end the night doing something I've never seriously done before: pray.

4 November 1995, Day 10

I watch myself watch the events of the day. The watcher watching me is thinking about someone far away from this place. The watcher on the set jots notes and jokes with the crew, just like any other day. Except this day is spent in hell.

SNAPSHOTS FROM THE UNDERWORLD:
In the background a glorious sunset after a day's hard rain; in the foreground, Bruce McDonald, his head half-shaven and caked with blood, facing the camera and ranting in quavering voice about being conned by Joe into making this fraudulent film and being shitkicked by skinheads.

A country road. The goat van in the foreground. Down the road Joe and Billy douse a large Nazi flag with gas, then set it alight and dance atop it, risking burns and making everyone nervous. When Bruce says "Cut!" Anne Simonet's inimitable Minnesota twang crackles over the walkie: "Heeey, theeyerz a goat heeyer."

A brown and white horned goat named Rainbow is led off the back of a pickup truck. Here he is at last, our symbol of artistic freedom. At least he will be once we've sawed him in half.

herbie's monster burger

Bruce sits in a kitchen chair as his head is completely shaved. All the long wispy hair, gone. He looks naked, vulnerable, like a raw egg that could break at the slightest touch. It's one more thing I can't quite believe he's gone through with.

Darkness. A large bonfire is built beside the house. Lights are set to illuminate the spooky trees and backlight the house. There is no music in this scene, but it is nonetheless the most operatic setting in the film.

Versions of glam. Julian wears top hat, tails, trousers, with no shirt, and thick black eye makeup over pancake white. Like a skinny white Baron Samedi. Hugh wears rubber-like pants and a silver shirt, thick eye makeup. Callum goes Vegas-glitz cowboy, in velour pants, shiny jacket, frilly shirt, and cowboy hat. Bernie wears a variation on the Leatherface look called for in the script: leather apron, fishnet stockings, leather jacket over this. Unbelievably long false eyelashes, a turn-of-the-century German army helmet with a point on top. Pyper goes for it clad in a cape, tinsel hair, baby doll makeup. The actress who plays Bucky's wife, Naomi, wears jodhpurs, jackboots, suspenders, a peaked military cap, chomps a cigar. Even our sound recordist Joe Schliessler is made up, kind of like Pyper in the tinsel hair and doll makeup. Only non-glam performer is Rainbow the goat.

Rainbow's handlers give Callum and John lessons in how to wrestle the goat onto his side. They practice for about twenty minutes.

A scarecrow mount has been erected and backlit in the field. Julian stands upon it, his sleeves and pantlegs jammed with straw. Crew members are humming "If I Only Had a Brain."

Bruce stands across the bonfire with his brand new bald head, wearing a pair of round glasses, looking like a Nazi directing some sort of blood sacrifice on a moonlit night.

Come to think of it, he is directing a blood sacrifice on a moonlit night. Everything has an unreal air tonight. Even the air has an unreal air. The moon might as well be painted. The house shimmers, the tall grass seems to be alive. The white dog, sniffing around the place since yesterday, has become a wolf. The set throbs with energy and expectation. Maybe someone really did put acid into the coffee urn or something.

Julian steps onto the scarecrow perch and the night's filming begins. Joe walks past Bucky, looks up in horror to see him "come alive." Bucky wraps his spindly arms around him like a hungry ghost. Cut.

Then Joe becomes the scarecrow, his clothes stuffed with straw, and Billy "shoots" him with his guitar gun (a flare blasts off the neck).

The reverse shot of this has the bullet from the guitar gun blowing a hole through Joe's guts. So it's squib time again, only this time the charges are much heavier and are attached to huge blood packs on Hugh's (i.e., Joe's) belly and back. The explosive is set to go off. Bruce yells "Action!" A collective holding of breath on the set. Then a huge explosion at Hugh's midriff. Blood erupts out of him, front and back, Hugh screams "FUCK!" and topples off his scarecrow perch and lies motionless. A stunned silence, then people leap to him and a crowd forms. Catch sight of Christine, stricken, thinking holy shit, we've killed our star. There's an agonizing moment, then Hugh speaks at last: "Fuck me, that thing's got a kick." Then he's back on his feet explaining that the wind was knocked out of him from the impact. Bruce sends him into the house for a change of clothes so we can get on with the shoot.

The core of the acid movie: shots around the campfire

involving the goat. Someone puts on some music for atmosphere. Marianne Faithfull's version of "Working-Class Hero." The air is fogged by one of the art department guys. Pipefitter dances wildly in front of the house, waving a chainsaw over his head. The shadow he casts against the house is enormous. John and Billy lead the goat by the horns around the fire a couple of times, then tip him to the ground and pin him there. Rainbow strains and struggles to lift his head, finally resigning himself to the demands of the scene and lying there relaxed. John and the goat touch tongues in a bestial French kiss. Pipe dances his way forward with the chainsaw. Bucky dances like a wild magpie around him. Joe stands staring off into the distance like he's communing with the god of working-class heroes.

A guy arrives with some pizzas for the crew, sees what's going on, leaves in a quiet hurry.

You start with a joint, and before you know it . . .

A reverse shot: Pipe is sawing into the goat with the chainsaw, and a props person is spraying fake blood all over him from a spray bottle. Bruce turns to me and says that those critics who have hitherto found his movies to be soft at the core, should "suck on this."

Blood everywhere now. Bucky stands at the fire, holding the goat's severed head aloft. Okay, not Rainbow's head, but the head of a very similar goat, acquired from a butcher and stored in the freezer at the production office these last few weeks. (Rainbow is "wrapped" for the night and goes home with his handlers.) The props people soak the bottom of the frozen goat's head in hot water to make it steam, then spray it down with fake blood. Joe, Billy, Pipe, and John each walk up to Bucky, who spreads the goat's blood on their faces and chests. Then they enter a four-way embrace and spin in a tight circle, around and around, as close as they will ever be, from ritual to romance and back again.

4 November 1995, Evening

I call Siobhan from the hotel, tell her about my day. She tells me about another chat with her doctor, who said that the higher than normal chance of Down's is about one in five hundred, as opposed to the norm, which is one in many thousands. Not as bad as it sounded last night, but there's still cause for concern. Again I offer to fly home. Again Siobhan, who knows full well how much I love this freakshow, tells me to stay on. It's shameful, how easily I am talked into it.

5 November 1995, Day 11

All day long it's night. Pouring rain and dark, dark, dark. Joe is at the wheel of the goat van, Billy sits beside him. They're

herbie's monster burger

singing, "I'm tired of wakin' up tired, wakin' up tired, wakin' up tired..." The others are asleep in back. Bruce is up front with the camera. Silence. Headlights passing on the highway. Then Billy says *"Touch of Evil."* Joe thinks a second, says *"La Dolce Vita."* And so it goes, on down the highway, the movie game scene, until the inevitable "Cut!" from Bruce. A production assistant turns the hose off, putting a stop to the rain. Another kills the headlight contraption outside the van windows. The guys climb out of the van and stretch. The production assistants leaning on the outside of the van, rocking it to simulate movement during the scene, also take five. For the first and only time, we're faking it in a studio.

*

Another nightshoot freakshow, outdoors at Jericho Park on Point Grey. Picture a caterer's tent filled with skinheads in the darkness, trying to learn the words to a song in French, but the darkness makes it impossible to read the small print on the lyric sheets. The wind is howling, and even inside the big tent (which later blows down and tumbles across the lawn towards the beach) people have trouble getting purchase on a lighter flame to read by. So Rachel writes the words to the song out phonetically, in huge print, on a seat torn loose from a cheap wooden chair. Then she stands at the front of a large gang of skinheads and leads them through the song, a flashlight illuminating the lyrics for all to see.

The phonetic spelling of the words on the seat is priceless:

OH CANADA ... TERR-UH DE NOZE EYE-UH,
TON FRO AY SAN DAY FLERRON GLOR-EE-UH,
CARTON BRA, SAY PORTAY LAYPAY-UH,
EEL SAY PORTAY LA CRWAH,

TON EASTWAAR ATE OON AY-PO-PAY-UH, DAY PLOO BREE YAWNS EXPLWAH...

Then it switches back to English, with "God keep our land," etc., and ends with a rousing chant of "WHITE POWER!"

*

In tonight's scene, Hard Core Logo are in transit between Saskatoon and Edmonton. They pull into a campground for some free shut-eye, only to hear a large group of men singing the national anthem somewhere nearby. Director Bruce and the guys go to investigate and find a gang of skinheads standing around a campfire under a huge swastika flag, belting out the bilingual version of "Oh Canada," which ends with a Nazi salute and virile chant of WHITE POWER! A bizarre sight even for the Hard Cores, who have done and seen many strange things. John, whose brain is basically transmitting on an unknown frequency at this point, runs into the circle of skinheads and accuses them of hating people so much because they themselves lack self-esteem. The skinheads grab the guys and the film crew, kick the shit out of Bruce and shave his hippie hair. John somehow manages to steal the Nazi flag in the confusion. That's basically it. That's what we film. That's how sixty adults spend the evening. Neat, huh?

During a long boring stretch of scene blocking, I walk to a pay phone, call Siobhan, stand in the rain talking for an hour.

6 November 1995, Day 12

Big skookum punk in a black overcoat and mohawk sits with his face bloodied on the steps of Big Sid's, staring at the bottle of cheap rye between his boots. People step carefully past him on their way out of the club. They're all couples, paired up, happy, going off into the Edmonton night in search of the next party. Punk barely notices, lost in his black thoughts. Finally he gets to his feet, starts to walk away down the street. Pauses. Thinks. Turns around, heads back up this way. Out of nowhere a smile comes to his face. Eye contact. He walks up. "We were good," he says. "Enda the tour . . . I thought it was excellent. Get everything you need? Didja have a good time?"

"Yeah," you say.

"You 'n' me, we're buddies," punk says. "We're buddies." Takes a drag of his smoke, pulls a shot glass from his coat pocket, fills it from the bottle. Hands you the bottle. Toasts you.

"Time for one last shot?" he asks.

You shrug. Whatever. Camera's still rolling. Maybe he'll do something funny here.

"What's that thing they say? One last shot and salut . . . ?" Joe Dick raises the shotglass with one hand as the other reaches into his pocket and pulls out a gun . . .

*

Catch up with the crew at the corner of Hamilton and Pender after a long lunch with Turner, Porteous, and Allen Moy in Gastown. (Turner broke down and read the script after all; says he likes it.) Crew spent the day shooting around town, scenes from the opening of the film where John and Joe talk about the upcoming benefit concert for Bucky. Now it's six, dark on the street, time for the last shot of the day, which is to be the last scene in the film.

Bruce and Hugh are in the actors' trailer. Hugh is on the cellphone to Callum, who is in Winnipeg for the day, doing his duty on *My Life as a Dog*. "So I go backwards, then? So my knees don't hit first? . . . So I just relax . . . What if I hit my fuckin head? Well I dunno, I've never done this before . . . I'm not the Hollywood fag actor here . . ."

There's more to it than Hugh calling Callum for advice on how to fall down. The call is about Hugh getting some reassurance from the guy he trusts most about how to carry off the most important scene in the film. When Hugh hangs up he's in a black mood, would rather I wasn't there. He's getting methoded up and Bruce is the only one he wants to see. Bruce is going to put Hugh in a frame of mind that will carry him through the final scene, THE NEW ENDING. The ending that has caused all the panic, all the arguments. It is Joe Dick's last moment on screen.

Head into the legion on the corner for a beer with Karen and Christine. Porteous comes up from his office and joins us. A couple of old men sit at tables, legionnaires, I guess. There are plaques, banners, remembrances stuck all over the walls, for those who have fallen in battle.

*

Christine asks what's going on for the final shot. I never officially wrote it into the script (I did, but never printed it off) on the logic that *not* putting it in writing will keep ammunition out of the hands of those opposed to it. Bruce, Hugh, and I worked it out the other night. There's nothing to do but rehearse it on the street and shoot.

Small problem: Christine and Karen are still under the impression that Bruce has an alternate ending he can shoot just to be on the safe side. They are under this impression because he has told them that he will shoot an alternate.

herbie's monster burger

Stupidest thing I could possibly say (and do say): No, Bruce was never going to shoot an alternate. This is it. One last shot. And oh that magic feeling, nowhere to go. Enda story.

If Christine's face were a satellite weather map, you'd see all this clear sky suddenly blotted out by a huge swirling hurricane. She storms outside in search of Bruce. Karen subjects Keith and I to another lecture about the consequences of breaching entertainment contracts, and, to paraphrase, how this horrific and downbeat ending could potentially land us in the shit. Keith kicks me repeatedly under the table. Shoulda kept my big fat mouth shut.

*

What all the fuss is about: Night of Day 2, an eternity ago. Hugh comes up to our suite with a little suggestion about the ending:

"I wanna die at the end of the picture."

Hmmm. Don't know about this. We tried killing both John and Billy in earlier drafts, and it never seemed to work. Somehow, we never thought of killing Joe. He's the Energizer Bunny of the bunch, the one most likely to just keep going and going and . . . it just didn't seem to be in the cards. Hugh persists. His Joe Dick is an all-or-nothing guy, true enough. Might work. We kick it around and start to see the logic of it, start talking ourselves into it. I draw the usual blank stare when I offer, "A bullet in the head would furnish an appropriate thematic closure to the film, the perfect culmination of the rock 'n' roll myth."

Hugh: "Whatever. I just think I should fuckin die at the end."

I do like the fact that the very climax of the film would be the last shot itself. No dénouement. Just a stone cold ending, with nowhere left to go but home. Is it maybe too abrupt though? We kick it around some more, consider the impact. Finally Hugh crashes, satisfied that we'll see the light. Bruce and I have another B&B (we're in the late-night liqueur habit here). Long silence.

Me: "Lots to think about, huh?"
Bruce: "Yup."
Me: "So what do you want to do?"
Bruce: "I say we kill the fucker."

*

Christine's objections to the new ending have been rooted in valid, well-reasoned artistic concerns. She has been saying for days that Joe Dick is a cockroach, a survivor. He'll fuck people over in order to get what he wants, to keep on going. It simply doesn't make sense she says, for him to blow his brains out in the final frame. Can't say I disagree with her logic. I'm still of two minds myself. It's just that deep down I know I'll follow the more bloody-minded of these minds.

*

There's a scene that comes early, before the Rock Against Guns benefit, where Joe talks about mythic rock 'n' roll deaths, casting Bucky's mere maiming as a denial of his rightful place in the tragic pantheon:

>   JOE
> There was Chapman shooting Lennon. Rock
> 'n' roll assassination, right? Cobain
> does himself. Rock 'n' roll suicide. Then
> Marvin Gaye . . . guy's own father blows
> him away. Total psychodrama. But all rock

herbie's monster burger

> 'n' roll deaths, right? Then there's
> Bucky . . . not killed, just crippled.
> Man was robbed, you know what I'm sayin?

Joe Dick's death wish is already in place in the script, lying in wait, a challenge to be taken up. The Joe Dick in Turner's book and in the script is a very realistic creation. It's only now, seeing him and the others transformed into larger-than-life beings on film, that it makes sense to see him as a mythic figure who "deserves" to die in high style.*

*

One last shot: Joe Dick stands before the camera, knocks back the scotch in his left hand and in a flash he raises his right hand, puts the gun to his temple and

BANG!

a thin cable of blood follows the bullet out the other side of his head. Joe goes down hard, as dead men tend to do. Tinkle of shot glass breaking. You stand there gagging on the heart that's leapt into your mouth . . . someone screams for an ambulance . . . and you know it's too late for that. You know there's nothing left to do but roll some credits.

*

It is, let's face it, a horrific ending. Not a joking matter. A tragedy. Joe Dick kills himself while talking to the camera. It's an emotional jolt most people are going to have difficulty

---

* I later discover that Hugh misread the passage on film, forgetting the stuff about Bucky being robbed by being "merely" wounded. Hopefully enough of the sense will survive for the ending to work thematically and not come out of nowhere.

———————— hard core roadshow ————————

What all the fuss is about.

coming to terms with. Intellectually, it's the ultimate interruption of the discourse between subject and audience. Either way, it's a slap in the face.

As the crew wraps for the day, there are tensions between Bruce and Christine. Hugh, who has just gone through several jarring takes, has a spooked guy-on-a-desert-island look. He heads back to the trailer, slams the door.

*

In the evening it's off to Danny Nowak's place for a party. Tomorrow's a day off, and having just killed Joe Dick, everyone is ready to go crazy. One fun thing about it: we're going to screen the dailies from Bucky's farm in Danny's basement.

It turns into a huge party, with far more than crew people showing. I think Bernie put the word out, so we've got the gals from Lick the Pole here, all these others I've never seen. Tons of beer, practically a full case for everyone here. Crew's

— herbie's monster burger —

in a drinking mood, it would seem. All night long people debate whether this ending will work, whether or not it's a mistake. Most people are excited by it and think it will work, but there are more than a few detractors. I suspect this debate will continue for some time.

Late at night we drunkenly watch the rushes from the farm — all the Bucky acid movie stuff. Everyone's looking forward to this, thinking we're going to be seeing the raw material for a surrealist masterpiece. It starts well, funny as it should be, one shot coming after another. No sound. There's Hugh with his guts being blown out, there's Callum shooting a flare off his guitar neck, there's Julian dancing around the fire. It's hypnotic to watch, a little stranger than I'd imagined it would be. A lot more disturbing. Several minutes into the sequence everyone has gone deathly quiet. No one is laughing by the time Callum and Pyper are seen leading the goat around the bonfire, wrestling it down, waiting for Bernie to come buzz its head off with his chainsaw. Somehow I thought it would be funnier. Sit there with Bruce and Reg and we all just repeat the words, Holy Shit.

When the lights go up the party-hearty atmosphere has been dragged way down, and things just get weird and ugly from here to the bitter end. Like coming down off bad acid. Bottles get broken. Someone gets thrown out. Someone pukes on the stairs. Someone passes out. People trickle out. Catch a ride to the hotel with Porteous. Another late end to another night in Hard Core Logoland. I'd hate to wake up to Danny's mess. I feel a cold coming on.

7 November 1995

Day off. Cold's come on strong. Can't breathe. Can barely move. Bruce has a brutal cough of his own now. Was bound to happen. What you get for killing heroes and defenseless animals. Today's weather: near-Biblical rainfall. I do laundry. Hot bath. Call Siobhan. Sleep.

8 November 1995, Day 13

Still with this ripping head cold. Hearing's a bit off, like my ears are attached to someone else's head.

An alley off Hamilton Street, between Pender and Hastings. Just down from the legion where Joe Dick killed himself the other day. We shoot the opening scene where Joe gives the opening "fuck you" anarchy speech about what HCL stand for. Here Bruce interviews Hugh off the cuff and elicits some great ad-libs. He has discovered that one of the best ways to get natural performances is to add unscripted questions to scripted interview moments. Many of the film's best moments have come out of these extra questions, where the spontaneous answers create an energy and truth such moments might lack if they were being "acted."

In the afternoon we head to North Vancouver and the Capilano Suspension Bridge, a last minute location to replace Wreck Beach, the Vancouver nudist beach where we had planned to have John and his girlfriend Celine facing the camera naked, holding hands, just like John and Yoko. They were to talk about John's feelings about the reunion tour, and we were to get the feeling that Celine is the one who calls all the shots in the relationship. There was to be a game of nude beach volleyball going on in the background.

Well, it's just too cold and wet today for this. It'd look far too strange having nude people on a beach whose breath you can see in the air. The advantage of the suspension bridge is that we can show John hanging in mid-air above a dramatic gorge with water thundering below, a perfect visual complement to one of his diary entries about a flying dream in which he falls and graphically anticipates the moment of impact and death. Without Hugh and Bernie around, things are downright tranquil as we spend the rest of the day shooting John talking to the camera on the footbridge.

We finish early. Back to the hotel. In bed by seven.

9 November 1995, Day 14

The three actors' agents have caught the buzz on what a great film *HCL* is turning out to be. They think that this "making of" film that Danny Salerno is doing is now very important. Now they want money from Danny for their clients to "appear" in his documentary. Christine mentions that one of the agents even heard that I was publishing a production diary, and was exploring ways to wrest some cash from me when I get a book deal. Wish I had an agent like that.

*

Today it's Bruce and the art department. Shooting black limbo stuff in the studio against black backdrops: spinning clocks, a life preserver ring, a spinning CD case, a Hard Core Logo album cover, etc. Visuals that will be cut into the film here and there to punctuate the narrative. The most interesting thing that gets shot is a mock-up of a road at night. It is basically a black cylinder or barrel, fashioned out of card, tape, paint, and so on, which spins around. There is a yellow highway line painted up the middle of it. When this spins towards the camera, and two flashlight beams hit it in just the right way, it looks like a cheesy POV shot from a moving vehicle on a road at night. All this is painstaking work.

*

Tonight we blow off important scenes scheduled for our "Joe's kitchen" location. Bruce says we'll pick them up at a different location at the end of the day tomorrow.

I hope so. It's a scene where Joe convinces Billy to go on the tour. I've been rewriting it for days. It's a critical moment in the story. Billy can't just up and go; there must be resistance. It could be a game with Billy, to see how far Joe will go to get him to come on tour. I've tried versions where Joe has literally begged while Billy sits there magisterially, petulantly, "considering" it. Nothing seems to have quite the right ring yet, especially given the relationship Callum and Hugh have established onscreen. The main problem is that the scene contains information needed for the story, but isn't the kind of thing you'd see done "naturally" in a documentary. Yet we have to have this information, or there'll be a huge hole in the film.

10 November 1995, Day 15

Today we put the goat van on a picture trailer and film the skinhead hitchhiking scene. Though the scene is supposed to take place near Revelstoke, which is more than halfway to Calgary, we actually film it in the GVRD, a government rainforest park in North Vancouver.*

It is impossible for me to fit into the goat van with the actors and crew and equipment, so there's much waiting around in passenger vans with other crew members. My God, is it cold and boring here. Thus it's only a matter of time before we fall into discussing the inevitable and all-important Who Is Fucking Whom on This Production? Two trysts are

---

* The scene is later cut from the film, along with all the skinhead material.

---— herbie's monster burger ———

confirmed and two or three more are speculated on. This kills about an hour. Then the boredom returns. Then one crew member tells a funny story about another crew member (who shall remain nameless, in print anyway) who, on another film, was caught masturbating one day in the empty production office. This leaves us all shrieking and really brightens up the otherwise dull day. Especially when we see the poor guy.

*

Late in the afternoon we head back into the city to the Tiki Room at the Waldorf Hotel on East Hastings. It's as if this hotel, which has been here since the 50s, has been waiting all this time for the 90s cocktail music scene to arrive. The lounge we're shooting in has a domed ceiling painted midnight blue, with pinlights for stars. There is a thatch-roofed bar. Woven-grass wallpaper. Black velvet Polynesian nudes hang on the walls. Bruce has people dress up in cocktail wear for background. Hugh and Callum sit at the bar in the foreground. The setting and mood cut hard against anything else in the film and I fear a mistake is being made in the interest of a lily-gilding Bruce-McDonald moment.

This is where Bruce has decided to film the former "Joe's kitchen" scene, where Joe talks Billy into going on tour with the band. Problem is, it really doesn't make documentary sense for the camera to be here during a private moment between two old friends.

Bruce clearly has something in mind here. He has Callum and Hugh improvise take after take around the scene I scripted, cutting them loose, hoping they'll come up with some cool material that will disguise the thoroughly plodding purpose of the scene. They go for broke, trotting out private jokes, doing shtick arising out of their own friendship. After a couple of hours, when the scene is no longer recognizable, I split, feeling tired and depressed.

On my second B&B back at the hotel it occurs to me that Bruce is totally right to set the scene in the most artificial environment he could find to flaunt the fact that *HCL* is not real. If the scene was going to look obvious and forced in our documentary style, why not go hard in the other direction and turn Joe and Billy's private world into a candy-colored la-la land. Eventually I also admit that Hugh and Callum improvised a better scene than I was able to write.

I call Siobhan. No answer. I'm tired but want the company of people who have nothing to do with this film. I meet friends for drinks and try to talk about anything but *HCL*, but find myself explaining how I ended up a screenwriter, seeing as I left this city nearly ten years ago without any apparent talent. Aside from my abiding love for films, a major reason why I wanted to write screenplays, and perhaps someday direct them, was that I thought this would be easier and less daunting than doing the thing I've most wanted and feared to do: write novels. *Easier.* Christ.

11 November 1995, Day 16

We shoot Billy's radio interview scene from Edmonton. Another scene I've been dreading. This is where we learn that Billy has been invited to become a permanent member of Jenifur after all, and that in spite of his promise to Joe to renew HCL, he's going to leave. The question, scriptwise: should Billy actually tell the whole world on-air that he is leaving HCL? Or should we leave the question open to create some suspense about Billy's decision during the final show?

I'd intended to rewrite the scene last night, but went out and got drunk instead. I arrive late on the set to find Bruce,

---------------- herbie's monster burger ----------------

Callum, and Dean Paras, the young actor playing the radio interviewer, already rehearsing the scene. The way they've worked it out, the interviewer asks Billy about the future of HCL on-air, but by way of answer Billy silently shows him a fax from L.A. renewing the Jenifur offer. The interviewer reads the fax and gets excited, wants to talk about it on air. Billy refuses to finish the interview, and he even asks Bruce the director if he'll be cool and not tell Joe. This suggests that Billy has not made up his mind about leaving Joe yet. But why show up for a radio interview, then refuse to talk? The scene doesn't make sense unless Billy drops the bomb on-air.

I discuss this for several minutes with Callum, who is dead-set against playing the scene as written, with Billy callously telling the world he's leaving HCL for good after tonight's show because he's got a better offer somewhere else. I suspect Callum doesn't want his character to openly betray Joe here for fear of looking like an asshole. Like any other movie star, he knows that he "is" his role in the eyes of the public.

When we shoot it, the point of the scene sort of comes across, but it could have come through stronger if Billy had stabbed Joe in the back on-air.

*

We wrap Vancouver. That's it for scenes here. The crew strikes the set at the radio station. Cables are hauled out, equipment is loaded into trucks. Bruce, Hugh, Callum, John, Bernie, and I check out of the hotel. I store my stuff at the production office. There's a catered lunch in the parking lot. After this the crew photo is taken by our stills photographer, Liane Hentscher. We arrange ourselves along the side of the goat van. Liane sweetly prompts us to say cheese. We all give the finger. Snap. A portrait for the ages.

*

We hit the road in the afternoon. The convoy: the Headstones' tour bus, which we've rented from Hugh's manager Joe Bamford, and which about a dozen of us ride on, including Bruce and the cast. The grip truck, which contains all the lights, rigging, and camera gear. The sound guys have their own van. There's the craft service van. The goat van. Anne Simonet comes in her car. Danny Salerno and his crew have their own van. We pull out and head east, into the Fraser Valley, bound for Hope. I talk with Susan Lambie, our script supervisor, about dialogue changes throughout the course of production. She's had to scramble to track them all. Her script copy is covered with neatly printed ad-libbed obscenities.

*

Best clean ad-lib in the movie: Hugh to camera in an unscripted interview moment: "Billy wants the models and limousines; I'm happy with the hookers and taxicabs."

*

Some unbleachable ad-libs and off-camera insults collected over a few days:
"Ya fuckin felcher."
"Fuck you ya fuckin fuck."
"Fuck me."
"Fuckin cocksuck felcher."
"Felch my brown spider, ya freak."
"Joe, fuckhead that he is . . ."

herbie's monster burger

"Yer such a cu-ontrary motherfucker."

"No you shut the fuck up ya fuckin loser."

"I'm an asshole because they're all pricks."

"I love that motherfucker. That motherfucker was robbed. It's payback time. I owe him, this is for him. Now couldja turn that fucker off?"

"That would make you a kinduva cunt, wouldn't it?"

"Pro gash."

"Pipefelcher."

The filth that tumbles from the mouths of our stars. On the tour bus, a few of us (now largely inured to the unending onslaught of obscenity) work out the foul language currency in this film. Five fucks to a motherfucker. Five motherfuckers to a cunt. Four cunts'll get you a felcher. Now what is a felcher, exactly? Bernie explicates the term. Even I have minimum standards and won't reproduce the definition here. Suffice to say that the practice of felching involves suction . . .

Okay, damn the torpedoes. A felcher is he who sucks the semen out of another man's anus. Use of a straw is optional.

More on language. While the script itself contained about 150 variations of the word "fuck" (an outrageously high fuck-count as my work goes), the finished film is likely to have about a thousand. This is no exaggeration. To me, fuck is a sharp, useful, effective word when properly used. Fuck is a flyswatter smacking you in the face. It gets your attention. Screenwriters love it, makes them feel like their dialogue is real, that it pops. But wall-to-wall profanity with fuck as verb, noun, and adjective devalues your carefully selected foul language and flattens your dialogue overall. I fear that fuck may not be worth a fucking peso by the time we're fucking done here.

─── hard core roadshow ───

*

East of Abbotsford we find a nice spot to shoot the scene where Joe stops the goat van and dresses the guys down out on the road. The sun is just going down and the moment is right for a dawn scene (sunrise and sunset being interchangeable in film production). The spot we've chosen has a sightline where Danny Nowak can frame the mountains out of the picture to give the illusion that we're in the Prairies. All we need is permission from a dairy farmer to park our vehicles in his driveway and shoot the scene in front of his place.

Shooting a band meltdown on "the Prairies."

The farmer's response: "Gawlee, a movie? Sure, go ahead." He summons the rest of his family (wife, three small blond children) to come watch. They are just so incredibly wholesome, these people, like Ned Flanders and his family. They settle into lawn chairs on the driveway. The kids squirm in their seats, oh so excited to have a big film shooting right here in front of their house. There'll be bragging rights over the neighbors, no doubt about it. This is the scene they witness:

EXT. ON THE PRAIRIE HIGHWAY — DAWN

JOHN, BILLY, and PIPE are lined up in the glare of the headlights. JOE paces up and down past them. "Who the Hell Do You Think You Are?" is playing from the stereo in the van.

> JOE
> Let's move a few things into the open. Pipe: Hotel guy in Regina hauled me aside at the desk this morning, said you took a shit on the pillow, wiped your ass on the bedspread. The fuck's that? Uncool, man.

PIPE manages to look both defiant and embarrassed.

> JOE
> John: Your writing. It's putting us on edge man. You lost your pills, right? 'Cause we can see you fueling something dangerous.

> JOHN
> Dangerous.

> JOE
> Just stop it, okay? You got to relax. We got a few days left.

                    JOHN
What do you know about dangerous? DANGER!
DANGER! WHOOP WHOOP WHOOP WHOOP!

JOHN starts away. JOE grabs him, smacks him.
JOHN is shocked.

                    JOE
. . . Okay? I mean it, John, as your
friend I need you to get a grip. Okay?

Tears welling in John's eyes. A pause.

                    PIPE
What about Billy. Doesn't he get a
spanking too?

                    JOE
True Bill. Guess we're gonna can the
fuckin star trip, eh?

                    BILLY
              (walking away)
Or you'll what . . . bite me? . . . fuck
me? Ya fuckin fuckup.

                    JOE
Fuck you.

BILLY wheels around, starts shouting.

                    BILLY
You are a MAJOR FUCKUP! You were fucked
up last night, got all our money ripped
off, you were fucked up the night you
fuckin bit me, you were fucked up the

night you destroyed our career . . . YOU
ARE FUCKED UP EVERY TIME YOU GO OUT OF
YOUR WAY TO FUCK ME!!!
        (to John)
That honest enough for you, John-boy?
        (to Pipe)
And fuck you too!

                PIPE
Yeah well fuck you, Mr. Rock Star No More.

The actors find ways to cram twenty or thirty more fucks into the scene. We do several takes. I look over at the lawn chair gallery in time to see the farmer, shocked and appalled, dragging his brood out of earshot. The kids want to stay and watch. There are stern words, a spanking, tears. Strangely, the farmer says nothing to us at all. Perhaps he doesn't know where to begin. It occurs to me that one of us might have had the decency to warn him that the scene might be inappropriate for young ears, but . . . naah. This late in the shoot it feels like one of the tamer scenes we've done.

We wrap for the night and drive on to the town of Hope, polishing off a bottle of brandy along the way. Hugh and Callum lock themselves in the back room of the bus, leaving the rest of it to the rest of us. Their unabashed fascination with each other continues.

*

The chain-smoking on this crew. By now my voice is getting to sound like an old lawn mower. Or like Bernie. Bruce is hacking his way through the day, but smoking a pack and a half anyway. The actors have butts hanging out of their mouths during every take. They must be up to about three packs a day each. Except for John, who actually quit a few days ago and is sticking with it. The others think him insane for trying this in the middle of an intense shoot.

Bruce and Danny Nowak light up on the tour bus.

12 November 1995, Day 17
Hell's Gate & Cache Creek, B.C.
Most of the crew went out last night to the only club in town, and most of them seem to be paying for it this morning. I climb onto the tour bus early in the morning to find Bernie already smoking a joint in back. Gearing up for another day on the job.

We drive up the Fraser Canyon, bound for Hell's Gate. The same route Bruce and I took nearly a year ago when we were out here casting and location scouting. We spoke then about how great it was going to be, shooting here during the summer under clear skies, mountains visible. Right now,

herbie's monster burger

outside, the snow is blasting out of the sky, you can barely see a thing, same as last January. Hugh stretches out on the long bench in the front of the bus. Bernie sits next to him and rubs his chest. Signs of tenderness among our leads as things wind down.

We spend much of the day parked at a Hell's Gate truckstop as the guys shoot the band's first fight-in-the-van scene, where Pipe freaks out at Joe for not waking him at Herbie's, his favorite hamburger joint on earth. It's a long scene, and though it sounds simple enough, it's tough going. Pyper is actually driving the thing back and forth on the slush-covered road, through tunnels, as loaded logging rigs and trailers of wrecked cars barrel past. Bruce, camera crew, and the sound guys are crammed in back, filming the scene. Rachel and others follow in other vehicles, for safety reasons. They go back and forth on the highway for hours and hours and do something like thirteen takes to get the master shot alone. Which leaves me with everyone else hanging out in this parking lot waiting.

Finally, with daylight running out, the crew packs it in and we drive on to Cache Creek, arriving in complete darkness to shoot further scenes in a snowy field next to a crumbling horse barn. Here the guys get back into their glam costumes and we shoot pickups for the acid sequence at Bucky's farm. Throughout the crew a sense that the end is drawing near, so a holiday atmosphere reigns and practical jokes abound. Hugh even takes a leak into a Cup-A-Soup which is slurped down without complaint by an unwitting crew member.

We wrap at midnight and head to the only bar in town to party our asses off, as this is our last night together as a crew. Christine has made it easy, pre-buying trays of food, some full bottles of scotch and vodka and many jugs of beer.

Nervous looks from the bar staff as we commandeer the DJ booth and dance floor. Goes okay for a while, but soon we've killed off all the booze, eaten all the food, the staff want to go home, and they kick us out when the speakers blow halfway through "Highway to Hell."

The thing is, Cache Creek has no idea how young the night feels to us.

*

Another scene that won't make it into the finished film.

```
INT. A ROOM AT A CACHE CREEK MOTEL - NIGHT

A wild party in progress, bodies pack the room
from end to end. There are two twin beds, and
partyers dance atop them. In the corners men
and women grope each other. Everywhere else,
people dance with wild, lascivious gyrations to
Stevie Wonder's "Superstition," which blares
from a cheap boombox.

A phone rings and rings, barely audible over
the whooping and screaming.

                              CUT TO:

THE BATHROOM

where the tub is filled nearly to the rim with
vodka, and partyers simply bend over and suck
it out with straws.
```

─────────────── herbie's monster burger ───────────────

                              CUT TO:

A CLOSET

where two crew members are having sex.

                              CUT TO:

THE ROOM AGAIN

as more and more people cram their way onto the twin beds and play a punk version of Hitchcock's <u>Lifeboat</u>, where the object is for as many people as possible to pogo as hard as possible without falling off. Then, inevitably, a pair of loud CRACKS are heard. The bedframes shatter, and beds and bodies collapse to the floor. A CHEER goes up from the partyers, who keep on dancing on the lopsided beds. Meanwhile the smoke is so thick that visibility is down to three or four feet.

Bruce throws his head back and howls like a coyote. Shawn picks up the still ringing phone and speaks Cantonese into it, then hangs up with a shrug.

Rancid starts playing on the boombox, loud. Violence becomes an option. The transport guys offer to go out to the truck for some power tools and tire irons to "fuckin do the place."

We suddenly become aware of an urgent KNOCKING at the door.

───────── **hard core roadshow** ─────────

Bruce pulls it open. It is the woman who owns the motel, in her bathrobe, her face pinched with rage, her hair like a sea sponge. We cannot hear exactly what she says, but it seems she's threatened to get her shotgun if we don't desist this minute.

                    BRUCE
What're ya gonna do? Shoot us?

                  MOTEL LADY
If I have to.

*

Bruce and I are sharing yet another double room. We're tired but not too tired after the big party. Nothing on TV. It's three in the morning.

We hear the gals in the next room, talking, giggling. Sounds like raunchy girl talk, the stuff that never gets said in front of guys. Bruce and I hold our breath the better to hear. No good, walls are just thick enough to muffle the words. Spot some motel drinking glasses wrapped in paper at the sink. Unwrap them. Place them against the wall, place our ears against them. This is better for volume, but worse for clarity. Sounds like four women from our crew and we know they're talking crew gossip, tasty stuff, with little sidebar forays into sex and death. It's too muffled, we can't quite make out the words. Better to just bang on the wall and tell 'em to speak up.

13 November 1995, Day 18, Cache Creek

Seven in the morning, breakfast at a local spoon called Chums. One glassy-eyed crew we got here. Hangovers on

――――――― herbie's monster burger ―――――――

some, others still drunk. Everyone talking in unnaturally deep smoke-shredded voices, sounding like the bastard children of Brian Mulroney and Harvey Fierstein. Clatter of cutlery might as well be trains colliding. Couple of the women on the crew tell Bruce and me about these strange noises coming from our room last night, as of drinking glasses being placed against the wall the better for a pair of sad cases to eavesdrop. We shrug, can't imagine what they're talking about, seeing as we were sound asleep resting up for today.

To Hungry Herbie's ("Home of the Monster Burger") where we shoot the scene where Joe shows John and Billy the cassette tape recorded at the live benefit show, a tape he plans to sell at concerts for extra cash. In the middle of a shot the motel lady barges in and she's hopping mad about the two broken beds. Zones in on our coordinator Erin Smith, demands that she come back with her to survey the damage. She wants to rub somebody's nose in it. Erin smiles, says "It's okay, we take your word for it." The motel lady demands seventy-five bucks for each of the beds. Erin smiles, "Cash or cheque?"

"Cash will do," says the motel lady, deflated. You get the sense she wanted the fight, not the money. She has to settle for the parting shot, "If you're ever back in Cache Creek, stay away from our motel."

We get the shots we need and move on. Plan is to backtrack to Hell's Gate and pick up some shots from yesterday, then do some more shooting at a roadside fruit stand where the guys buy Pipe the food he missed by sleeping through the Herbie's stop. So we all pile into the various vehicles and head on down the road.

*

Now I can understand the residents of small towns like Cache Creek feeling put upon by groups of invaders like movie crews, who have a tendency to flash their money around and lord it over the locals. The resentment makes perfect sense. I'd completely understand if the motel lady had, say, a strapping brute of a son who came into our party last night and threw a few crisp punches to disperse us. But what I can't understand is the actual form of revenge some jerkwater Jethro took on us for all the trouble we caused.

The tour bus arrives at the fruit stand back at the north end of the Fraser Canyon. Most of the other vehicles arrive. Then we wait for the goat van to arrive. We wait some more. And we keep waiting. It doesn't arrive. Someone is sent back up the road to check on it. A while later he comes back and tells us about the accident.

One of our sound guys was driving the goat van down the highway when it began to shudder and sway in the rear. Then the back end dropped with a screech of metal as both rear wheels flew off. The van bounced and scraped its way down the highway, nearly flipping over. The wheels went skipping ahead on their own, almost taking out a couple of oncoming cars. The van finally gouged its way to a stop. The driver was shaken, but he could easily have been killed, as could others on the road.

Two wheels do not fly off on their own. Our guess is that some redneck took exception to us last night, either at the bar or the motel, and decided to "fix us" by removing all the lug nuts from the rear wheels of the goat van.

*

We shoot the scene at the fruit stand where Joe picks out fruit for the angry Pipe. Then a final scene, completely ad-libbed, with the guys sitting on a picnic table at the side of the highway. Here each of the guys introduces himself to the camera, and Joe lays out the pecking order within the band. Not surprisingly, this mirrors exactly the reality of the four actors' relationship. Joe and Billy are numbers one and two, though Joe allows that these are interchangeable positions. Pipe is number three and John is four. Pipe would be four, but for the fact that John is usually living in a world of his own and not necessarily bucking for more respect or status within the group as Pipe does. This is also true of the actors themselves outside the filming.

With the scene finished it's time for Pyper to go. He has to get to the airport and a flight for L.A, where he begins work on a big-budget pilot for Paramount tomorrow. There are tears in his eyes as he says good-bye to Hugh, Callum, and Bernie, to Bruce, to me. Feels like we're losing a family member. He gets into Anne's car, then he's gone.

*

The goat van is towed back to Cache Creek and deposited in the parking lot next to Chums. Christine informs a group of RCMP officers about the van accident and the likely sabotage, but they don't seem to be overly concerned about it and look at us as if to say, well what did you expect?

We spend the rest of the afternoon shooting Poor Man's Process in the crippled van, picking up various interior driving shots. This will complete main unit filming.

Snow and sleet all day. Spend part of the time watching the filming, part of the time wandering around the town (reading sabotage in the faces of everyone I see), part of the time drinking tea in the tour bus. Late in the day, Bruce decides

Shooting in the goat van.

to put me in a scene. Ah, my cameo at last. I am to be a body double for the departed Pyper. I will sit in the foreground, in John's fringed buckskin jacket, writing in my (John's) diary. Pipe looks at me with suspicion in the background and asks what the hell I'm writing anyway. Nothing, I say. Road stories. My off camera dialogue will eventually be overdubbed by Pyper. All that is visible of me is my hand as it writes. Appropriate, no?

*

A final scene with Callum. Bruce has him lean back in the goat van and simply answer more questions in character. When this is done Bruce summons Hugh and Bernie to the van for what they think is yet another scene. They arrive grumbling. Here we all are: Bruce, Callum, Hugh, Bernie, Christine, Rachel, Danny Nowak, Joe Schliessler, me. Bruce nods to Rachel. Rachel grins and says the magic words, "That's a wrap."

And that's that. We scream our heads off, throw our arms around each other. Bruce calls for cheers for each cast and crew member. As we climb from the van, Bruce grabs my coat, pulls me close, gives me a big bear hug. We congratulate each other. Hard to believe this is it, it's over. Production has been sort of an epic journey. And yet, with this eighteen-day main unit schedule, it's a mere hiccup between the summer of '94, when I began writing, and the fall of '96, when the film will most likely be released.

Danny Salerno comes up with his cameras and asks how it feels, here at the end of this journey. It feels like being interviewed in the dressing room after winning the Stanley Cup. I tell him what I've learned on this film, about making movies, directing actors, scene blocking and coverage, all this technical stuff. I talk about the more important stuff I've learned, mostly from Bruce — about persistence, stubbornness, focus, nerve, attitude. I've learned that there are few things harder than making good films, and that the odds against ever making something lasting, interesting, or important, are very high. I think we've beaten those odds here.

Bruce joins me in front of the camera and talks about his love for the actors who became Hard Core Logo, his love for this story. For him the journey is maybe half over. The film has to be cut and recut, effects and opticals must be added, sound must be mixed, the film must go to festivals and must be sold. There is a soundtrack album to attend to. There is a long way to go yet, for him and Christine and Brian and Karen and Reg, for other post-production types I haven't met and may never meet.

*

A final gathering at the back of the tour bus with Bruce, Callum, Hugh, Bernie. We listen to the tape of HCL songs, all the way through, one last time. And we belt the words out. Bernie sings loudest, performing for Salerno's camera. Hugh and Callum sit back, looks of sadness. I get the sense that if they could do it, they'd chuck their lives and be Joe Dick and Billy Tallent forever. Callum leans to Bruce and says exactly what everyone else is thinking: "I don't want it to end."

But it has to. Bruce, Christine, Danny, Rachel, and a couple of others are going on from here, shooting second unit footage to the east, into Alberta. The actors are finished, as are the sound guys and most of the rest of the crew. I am invited along on the extended road trip, but decide to return to Vancouver, take a breather, visit family and friends.

The tour bus pulls up at the local liquor store and we stock up for the trip south. Then we're on the road. The party extends through the whole bus, with production assistants, ADs, wardrobe people, actors, everyone, telling stories from films they've worked on. Fun for an hour or so. Then things get more subdued. Hugh takes a low bunk. Callum lies on the floor beside him and they face each other, talking in hushed tones. In the end, it's still love. Other bunks are staked out. I fall asleep in the back room, wake later to find the entire bus quiet, the lights out, everyone asleep, the upcountry snowfall outside the window giving away to valley rain as we approach Vancouver in the middle of the night.

17 November 1995, Vancouver

The news from Toronto is an enormous relief: Siobhan's test result came back negative. The complication is gone, the scare is over, the burden is lifted. A healthy baby is on the way, due in late April, around the same time *Hard Core Logo* is finished and ready for festival screenings.

Spent a few days relaxing, hanging out with friends, visiting my mother and relatives on Vancouver Island. For the first time since arriving here and plunging into work, there's been time to reconnect some old ties.

Today I go into the production office and hear the following story. As the second unit crew returns to Vancouver from the road shoot, they pause outside Cache Creek. Having had no satisfaction in the complaint about the sabotage to the goat van wheels last week, Bruce is unhappy. He procures a can of spray paint and decides to leave a parting gift for the town on its Welcome to Cache Creek sign, transforming it into Welcome to Gash Creek, with an anarchy A circle around the A in Gash. About twenty minutes later as the vans proceed towards home, they are pulled over by the RCMP and Bruce is arrested and charged with vandalism. He has a court date for December.* Guess this really does make him an outlaw filmmaker.

18 November 1995

The wrap party is held at a restaurant on Commercial Drive. I go alone, find the place packed. It's a glam theme party, and the getups run the gamut from 70s glam rock to Louise Brooks flapper, to various cocktail lounge looks. Hugh is the only cast member here. Bernie is back on Vancouver Island. John is in L.A. working on the pilot he's been cast in. Callum is working in Winnipeg. No sign of Bruce.

Bands have been brought in to play. A bed has been set up on the floor in front of the stage for people to bounce on, in

---

* The charges against Bruce were later dropped.

———————————— hard core roadshow ————————————

honor of our motel party in Cache Creek. The evening passes in a blur of laughter and nostalgia for the weeks we've all just spent together. Still no sign of Bruce, though. His no-show is the night's major disappointment. Okay, for me not the major disappointment. That honor goes to a fight I get into with a local musician, who in the middle of a perfectly friendly drunken conversation transforms into Jake La Motta and starts throwing punches. Ugly moment, comes out of nowhere. Possibly something I said set him off, but I can't figure out what. Maybe it's my eye makeup. Otherwise it's a fun night and when things start to wind down, Rachel invites a number of us back to her loft.

In the cab with Rachel and Christine, we speculate about Bruce's no-show.* For some reason the words "Bruce" and "parties" combine in my head in such a way as to prompt me to tell the gals that Bruce thinks film parties are for "bottom feeders." Had no idea how hurtful this would sound and it sort of lies there like a fat steaming turd. Of course Bruce doesn't think of his colleagues as bottom feeders. Must learn to curb this cruel and unthinking tongue of mine.

20 November 1995

To Comet Post to view the dailies from the last few days, plus the second unit footage. The stuff from the Tiki Lounge is as good as I feared it would be. John on the suspension bridge looks beautiful, his performance is quiet yet packs an emotional punch. Road shots of mountain goats, the goat van crossing Prairie landscape and winding through mountain passes, all suggest that the finished film will look in part like

---

* Still exhausted from the shoot, he ended up sleeping through it.

an epic travelogue. All the dailies, in fact, point up the fact that, nasty and black humored as this story is in places, we all got together and created a powerful love story. And now the baton is in the hands of Bruce and the editor.

Just before I leave this place for the last time Reg tells me, as if by way of warning, that any drastic cuts made to the film, to my favorite material, should not be taken personally. Of course you don't take these things personally. I suppose screenwriters and film editors, who sort of bookend the director, always come to this point. The next "draft" of the film takes shape in the cutting room, and it will inevitably differ in some ways from the script. The script is no longer the raw material, the printed film is. What worked on paper doesn't always work on film and things change during production. You just have to trust that the director and editor will assemble the best movie they can from the available footage.

Time to go. Got a flight to catch back to Toronto tonight. Final good-bye to the core team: Bruce, Rachel, Danny, Christine, Karen, Reg. One by one, hugs, kisses, handshakes. I reflect that finally, all the rewriting, second-guessing, debating, arguing, collaborating, breakthroughs, setbacks, thrills, have brought me to a point that has changed the way I view myself as a writer and as a person. What I have become is an insider, part of a gang, a family, drawn in from the cold of the writer's habitual isolation to share a vision and goal with others, to will a powerful and complex piece of work into being. I have a new sense of confidence, a feeling that I am now well-launched on a path I've wanted to be on for years. As with sex and drugs, the first experience is the most fraught. From here on out the prospect of doing it again and again and again seems like no big whoop.

So parting is sweet you-know-what, and I walk out the door wet-eyed, a little embarrassed to find myself humming the last words of the most mythologized rock band in history: "And in the end the love you take is equal to the love you make."

21 November 1995, Toronto
Red-eye back to Toronto gets me home at eight in the morning, where I am mauled by the lovelorn Scout. Siobhan is also happy to see me. I'm glad to be back, to get on with my life, build a family, settle back into the writing routine. But . . . I sit here tonight looking at my Rock Against Guns poster, my *Hard Core Logo* T-shirt, my now-tattered script copy, covered with notes. I think about late-night meals in the hotel bar with Bruce, Hugh, Callum, Pyper, and Bernie, about the heightened sense of urgency to every moment during production. It's going to be hard returning to civilian life.

23 November 1995
To the Midtown on College where I run into a friend I haven't seen in months. He smiles, puts out his hand, congratulates me. I thank him and tell him that, yeah, the film went really well, it was great to get it finished, best experience of my life and I can't wait to see the final product, we all think it's going to be amazing, plus things are really taking off for me career-wise and I'm very happy about it, blah blah blah blah blah. Only later do I realize, feeling a complete moron, that he was congratulating me on my impending fatherhood.

In the immortal words of George Jetson, "Jane, stop this crazy thing!"

5.

PLAYING WITH A FULL DICK

30 December 1995

Bruce has stayed on in Vancouver to edit the film with Reg. Christine and Karen have continued working at the financial and contractual end of things. Brian has done the same in Toronto, as well as overseeing other projects. Hugh went on tour with Headstones. Callum, John, and Bernie went on to other acting jobs. I ended 1995 back at square one, working on new material.

I began 1996 in a resolutionary frame of mind. Beyond the annual vows to buy an RRSP and take up fencing, a promise to write five pages of new work a day, no matter what, to battle my *HCL* withdrawal head-on. If I write twenty days a month, 240 days during the year, I'll have banged out 1,200 pages by the end of December. Of course, by the time those pages are rewritten several times, the grand output will probably be about three hundred pages of new material. Still, that's three films worth. A depressing thought, though: from today, nothing I am working on, alone or in collaboration, will likely go before the cameras during 1996. Takes too long to put the rest of the pieces together.

9 January 1996

Bruce returns from Vancouver with the skinny on the rough cut. It's looking really good, he says, though the film is running long at about 115 minutes. The cannibal video is too jarring to work as a title sequence after all; it's being dumped. We'll use it as a music video promo clip. If there's a problem at the beginning, it's a lack of clarity about who HCL are, and why this "documentary" is being made about them at all. He suggests I write some kind of new setup, maybe even using a narrator to set the scene.

Bruce goes on to explain that the film wants to be about the family dynamics created by Joe, Billy, John, and Pipe, to the exclusion of most elements from the outside world. It wants to be a melodrama, it wants to be a story about four men hurtling through a landscape they barely notice as they attempt to reconstruct themselves as a viable band.

Sounds like the film hasn't hit its stride yet in the editing room. I ask Bruce if he's happy with it at this stage, at least. He proves himself a visionary, eyes focused on the film as it might become, and says he's fucking thrilled.

2 February 1996, Vancouver

Flew out here to view a fine cut of *HCL*. Bruce and Reg worked long hours to get the film to this point, their "first draft." It runs at around 100 minutes, meaning many more cuts have been made in the last few weeks. Present at the screening are Bruce, Reg, Christine, Karen Powell, Paul Gardner (the executive from our Canadian distributor Everest), people from B.C. Film and Telefilm, me. Frayed nerves in evidence as we make small talk before the screening. My heart thumps. Everyone smokes. We settle in to watch.

It begins well, funny and punchy, with Joe's anarchy speech in the alley, then Joe and John talking about Bucky Haight and the upcoming benefit concert. But within minutes the film starts going flat. There's no sense of where Billy came from. The band hit the road, but it doesn't seem like such a momentous event. The scenes I wrote are happening more or less as I wrote them, but they don't grip me, I don't feel

———————— playing with a full dick ————————

connected to them. Some of the biggest story points, like the revelation that Bucky has healthy legs after all, fail to register. To make matters worse, the acid movie sequence at Bucky's has been shoved through a digital imaging grinder to create a pointless interlude of glossy, surreal, high-tech images that look like some techno band's video instead of the fucked-up low-tech "art film" I wrote in which Bucky leads the rudderless HCL back to the promised land via a ritual sacrifice. From here to the end the film is more downbeat and less funny than I'd hoped. Even without the skinhead stuff, scenes from Saskatoon on to Edmonton drag badly. I am gratified when the audience chuckles here and there at some obvious jokes and several of Hugh's ad-libs, disappointed when I gird myself for explosions of laughter at my funniest bits, only to get no reaction. I actually cringe at some scenes and feel like slinking from the room.

I am gripped by the feeling that the whole film is a stranger to itself, that it doesn't know what it wants or where it's going, that it is crying out for signposts and maps to tell us not only where the band are headed, but where the story is headed. I begin to wonder whether the weaknesses are due to the poverty of the writing or the way the film has been cut together. The structure is sort of there, but so many moments play flat. The actors' performances are terrific, but the way they are put to use fails to do them justice. The one thing that does play well is the ending with the gunshot to the head. It wakes me up from what has felt like a bad dream.

Is this movie any good? Fuck knows. Is it improvable? It has to be. Will it be as great as we'd hoped? Hard to say. To be honest, I came here expecting to be blown away by the most kick-ass rock 'n' roll movie ever made. Instead I'm left addled, disappointed, my head a jumble of complaints.

We gather in a boardroom to chainsmoke and talk things over. Most comments are carefully prefaced by acknowledgments of what a "good start" Bruce and Reg have made. Then people get honest and things turn nasty, it being human nature to gloss the good stuff and repeatedly go for the gullet on that which is deemed to suck. I look at Bruce and Reg, slumped in their seats, listening glumly as all these suits, arts bureaucrats, bean counters, and a know-nothing writer lustily kick away at their work. As I take my turn laying in the boot my heart goes out to them, knowing that they must feel much as I did during so many of last year's emasculating script meetings.

20 March 1996, Toronto

Bruce and Reg have returned to Toronto to continue editing in the War Room where Reg has set up his Avid. I've been keeping in fairly regular contact since the Vancouver screening. Some of my suggestions have been taken up, some haven't. Reg and I have had our share of spirited discussions about various aspects of the film. On some points we've agreed to disagree. On others, we're still squabbling. Bruce listens passively to these jaw sessions, his face composed in a sort of amused twinkle, careful not to publicly take sides (lest creative differences become personal ones), yet taking it all in, quietly deciding what to do for the greater good of the film.

We've added some things: I wrote some lines to be looped over various scenes to clarify the story. Bruce has filmed scratchy black and white archival shots of Bucky hammering on a guitar and screaming into a mike. He's flown to New York to film a testimonial from Joey Ramone about Bucky

—————— playing with a full dick ——————

The otherwise invisible hand
of Reg Harkema, film editor.

and the Hard Cores. Lots of little things have been tweaked, tightened, and boosted over the last month. Time once again to have a look at the whole film.

The screening takes place in the War Room for a small audience of people close to the project. Nerves. But when the film rolls, I am quickly caught up in the story. Right away I can see that this is a radical improvement over the fine cut. The pace is much faster at the beginning. Text flashes on screen, explaining who Hard Core Logo are, when they were formed, when they split up, what they're doing here. It's simple, clear and quick, a documentary device that shoehorns us into the movie right away. In fact, all the improvements seem to derive from documentary devices: voice tracks sourced out of one scene or interview now appear over visuals from other places, giving the film greater speed yet more depth, a more seamless blend of forward thrust and backstory. There are now shots of an animated map of Canada showing where the band's tour is headed. Dates and times are now posted on the screen, giving a clearer sense of the relationship between time and distance on the tour. The stakes are better defined, there's much more logic and dramatic tension throughout, even though the film is about six minutes shorter than the fine cut was. Above all, it's funnier. The essence of comedy is timing, and Bruce and Reg have the timing down very nicely throughout. After the screening most of the viewers are astounded at the reality of the film, at the power of the performances, the music, the story. The film has found its feet.

10 May 1996

Exhausting week, though more for Siobhan than for me. "Late April" came and went and we waited and waited. The word "overdue" was spoken many times a day. Finally, late at night on 6 May, Siobhan's labor began. Then lasted a grueling twenty hours. Finally, at 8:30 p.m. on 7 May 1996, our healthy and adorable daughter Emma Claire Baker joined the world of breathers.

She has a full head of brownish hair, lovely clear eyes, very kissable cheeks, Siobhan's nose, my cowlicks, her own unique character. We're all back home from the hospital, relaxing, resting up for the rest of our lives.

Only thing on today's agenda is the first big-screen full-sound look at *HCL* before Bruce, Brian, and Christine take off for Cannes with it in a couple of days. There's been a great rush to complete the sound mix, nail down opticals, fix color, and other fine technical points, and now the film is basically set. In the audience at the Deluxe screening room on Adelaide Street East are Bruce's filmmaker friends, producers, some press people, business people, Telefilm and OFDC people.

This time the film is even better and its energy just leaps off the big screen. Bruce and Reg have made further minor cuts, removing the last external impediments to a story which is now exclusively about the band and its internal problems. I do miss some of the cut material; there's a lot of good writing and acting that will never see the light of day now. But the film plays faster than ever, and in the main it is still funny, brutal, and sad. *Hard Core Logo* is not without its technical and dramatic flaws, but it is a powerful, interesting film and I'm happy with it. Happier, I think, than I could have imagined when I first picked up Michael Turner's book and wondered if it was even possible to squeeze a movie out of it. I still have some minor quibbles, as all writers do when their scripts are filmed, but I am confident that the best film that could be made has, in the end, been made.

27 May 1996

Variety reviews *HCL* at Cannes. The venerable trade paper's wise, discerning critic considers the film "bitingly funny " yet "surprisingly poignant," bound to "please hip auds." The acid movie sequence at Bucky's is called "a side-splittingly funny snapshot of stoner culture." High praise goes to Bruce's direction, the actors' performances, Danny Nowak's camera work, the Peter Moore/Swamp Baby punk anthems, and the script. Every word is positive. Is it a rave? Close enough. Have to wait until October, when the film is released, to see if anyone else agrees.

1 August 1996

Dinner with Bruce, Hugh, and Callum, ostensibly to reminisce about the production period of the film to help me beef up some of the earlier sections of this book. Problem is, none of us is inspired by the prospect of looking backward like this. We're all steaming ahead with new projects. Callum is just finishing another movie in town, and will be doing more film work still later this summer. Hugh is recording another Headstones album that will be out this fall. Bruce is directing some episodic TV and developing new projects. I've got several new projects on the go, including one with Bruce. The thing about people whose lives are project-oriented is that they are only interested in what they are doing now. Bruce says he's always being asked about the making of *Roadkill* and *Highway 61*, and his anecdotes always have an unreal quality, as if he were talking about someone else's life. So it is with Callum and Hugh tonight. We give reminiscence a half-hearted stab but it's no use. Last fall is all a blur. When I resort to the moronic "What was the funniest moment in the making of the film?" everyone says, "Christ, not that one" . . . So we call it quits.

12 August 1996

Feeling like I am now an authority on punk reunion tours, I attend the Sex Pistols' Filthy Lucre Live reunion show in a spirit of detached academic curiosity. The venue is the Molson Amphitheatre, same place I saw Hugh Dillon eat a burning cigarette last year.

The Pistols take the stage in a storm of lights and noise, then settle into an hour of infamous twenty-year-old, three-chord anthems. As expected, punk irony is on offer, but it is overshadowed by unintentional irony: the concert is at a family amusement park. The decibel level is low enough for senior citizens. Johnny Rotten engages in arena rock crowd manipulations of the "Hello Cleveland!" variety, favorably comparing us to American audiences (cheap, easy, and effective). Johnny still has the sneer, the mock magisterial gait, the lord of misrule presence, but he goes too easy on the crowd. I long for controversy. I want him to insult our politicians, pick a fight with someone, heap scorn on us for paying these obscene prices. But no, the band simply dispatch their obligation like seasoned pros and head backstage to count their money. I know for certain that there really is "no going home" when the kid in front of me pulls out his cellphone and actually makes a call during "Anarchy in the UK." On the way out I can't help thinking that Hugh Dillon, who swallowed his drummer's phlegm on this very stage last summer, kicks the shit out of Johnny Rotten as a punk frontman.

21 September 1996, Sudbury, Ontario

The girls ain't playing bingo, the boys are getting stinko. We had a bit to drinko this Sudbury Saturday night. David Griffith is over from Scotland for a spot of work and he's come north on this bender with Bruce, Brian, several filmmakers and critics, and me.

This takes some explaining. To the consternation and puzzlement of many, *Hard Core Logo* gave the Toronto Film Festival a miss, a "snub" that prompted much speculation in the local film community. Since *HCL* wasn't involved in the Toronto event, I also gave it a miss this year. Bruce promised the Vancouver Film Festival the North American Premiere. That festival was most pleased to have the film, as the hype around *HCL* has been getting hotter and hotter. Then a few weeks ago the Sudbury Film Festival quietly invited Bruce to show the film. Seeing no harm in it, Bruce accepted. Great move.

We've been flown up here, all expenses paid. We ride around town in white stretch limos. We are fêted and fed, we drink our faces off. We are treated like VIPs. We are given a high-profile Friday night screening. Who'd have thought the Hollywood dream would be alive and well and living in Sudbury, Ontario?

The theater, in a downtown mall, is packed. I sit beside Dave, who hasn't seen the film yet. By now I've seen it about a dozen times, so when all the opening remarks and introductions are over and the film rolls I simply study the faces around me, lifted towards the big screen, shining, smiling, transported. The faces laugh at the funny bits. They look thoughtful at the thoughtful bits. They look dumbfounded during the acid sequence. They look sad during the sad bits. They nod along when the band plays. They recoil in shock when Joe Dick does you-know-what at the end. They then leave the theater in a sort of daze, as if they've just been rudely jerked out of a collective hallucination.

A large group of us fade off into the night for a punk after-party at one bar, more drinks at another bar, still more drinks at the festival's hospitality suite down the hall from our rooms. It ends at five in the morning when the life of the party, a burly native Indian drag queen who appeared in our midst at some point, tokes down her last hash joint with us and splits. A few of us meet for a late, shaky breakfast this afternoon, spend the rest of the day and evening watching films. Then comes another party that goes on until three or four in the morning. By now we have consumed enough hard liquor and exchanged enough scabrous opinions with the prominent critics and filmmakers present (about films and filmmakers not present) to feel like we are among old army buddies.

22 September 1996

The day's near-suicidal hangovers are soothed by the news that *HCL* has won the festival's top prize for Best Film.

20 October 1996

Spent a couple of weeks in Vancouver with Siobhan and Emma, staying at Mom's place. Emma got to meet her grandmother, aunts, great aunts, and uncles for the first time. It was nice to relax out there, catch up with old friends I'd not seen much of on my last visits. Naturally, the main excuse for going to Vancouver was the screening of *HCL* at the Vancouver Film Festival. A screening which ended to wild applause.

There was a large party for the film at, of all places, the Starfish Room, where my string of bad luck continued when a power-tripping doorman refused to let me back into the party after stepping out for some fresh air. I later learned he was convinced that I was just some asshole trying to sleaze his way into the night's hottest party by claiming to be the film's writer, Michael Turner. A classic screenwriter moment.

We returned to Toronto on the night of the 16th, my birthday. Among all the messages on my answering machine is one from Brian Dennis, announcing that I've been nominated for a Genie Award for Best Adapted Screenplay. The film has been nominated for five other awards, including Best Picture, Best Director, Best Achievement in Editing,

Achievement in Sound, and Best Song. While I'm pleased to be among the nominees, I can't believe that none of our actors has been nominated. Guess the performances were too "real" to be considered acting by whoever makes the nominations.

On Friday October 18th *HCL* is released across the country. I buy a number of newspapers from around the country and cannot believe what I see: the reviews are nearly all raves, some so over-the-top that modesty forbids quoting them here. Okay, I'll quote just one: the *Montreal Gazette* calls *HCL* "the best rock 'n' roll movie in the history of rock 'n' roll movies." True or not (such judgments being very subjective) this is my wildest dream for the film. I float over to Bruce's office and we sit there going through the papers, surfing on this tide of praise.

It doesn't end there. Tonight I receive another message from Brian: the Vancouver Film Festival has just wrapped up. *HCL* has won the award for Best Canadian Film, and I've won their award for Best Canadian Screenplay. This comes with a much-appreciated cash prize that is supposed to go towards computer equipment but which I will more likely spend on rent, bills, and baby food.

28 November 1996

It had to be experienced, I guess. Bruce and Heidi, Brian, Reg, Sandy Kaplansky, Christine, Karen, Peter Moore and Swamp Baby, the sound guys, Siobhan and I — we all suffer through the Genie Awards ceremony. The Academy and the CBC, having learned from past experience that most people would rather give bone marrow than watch the Genie Awards on TV, decided that the whole bloody thing could be "got through" in one snappy television hour provided that the only awards televised were in the crowd-thrilling categories of Acting, Directing, and Best Picture. The untelevised section features low priority, boring, non-telegenic "craft" categories like Editing, Best Song, Sound, Musical Score, Costume Design, Art Direction, and Original and Adapted Screenplay.

This portion of the event is quickly over. Nominees are named in various categories. Reg and the sound guys from *HCL* remain in their seats as people attached to David Cronenberg's *Crash* make for the podium to collect the hardware. Then my category, Adapted Screenplay, is called. I hear my name along with the others. Smile, take a breath. Little squeeze on the wrist from Siobhan, a few looks of encouragement from my colleagues down the row. And then the winner's name is read.

One of my idols, David Cronenberg, wins for *Crash*.

Later, during the televised hour-that-feels-like-a-week, Bruce goes through exactly the same thing when Cronenberg is called to the podium to accept the award as Best Director. The Best Picture category comes last. By now we know it is not our year and none of us is shocked when Brian and Christine remain in their seats as the producers of *Lilies* stride triumphantly into the spotlight to collect the statue.

There is one bright spot during the night, and that comes when "Who the Hell Do You Think You Are?" from *HCL* wins in the Best Song category. This is shared by Peter Moore, Swamp Baby, and fittingly, Michael Turner, who wrote the words to the song when he wrote the book. When Peter steps to the mike for his thank-yous, he reads a statement from Turner, that says when he wrote the words to "Who the Hell" he had no idea that Ontario would elect Mike Harris as premier. This gets the only honest (and untelevised) laugh of the evening.

Afterwards, cocktails and shmoozing. A heartwarming quorum of wellwishers drift by to assure us that we were "robbed" in our various categories. Nice to hear it, but I don't think any of us really expected to win. Over the last decade or so, good filmmaking in Canada has become synonymous with art film. You make a piece of cinema verité in which four guys strap on guitars, spit, swear, do acid, and hint cryptically at past homosexual acts, and no matter how sophisticated the filmmaking, Academy voters are likely to view it as a work of low culture unworthy of their votes. At least you know it's an interesting film year when the safer choices for the big prizes feature stylized gay prison sex and car crash sex fetishism.

6 December 1996

Again and again since the film's release, friends, strangers, and interviewers have asked me one question more than any other: how much of *Hard Core Logo* (or *Logo* as its most ardent fans now call it) is actually scripted? People find it hard to believe that a film so naturalistic, so "real," so seemingly accidental could possibly have been mapped out on paper before coming to life on screen.

Most people are probably thinking of dialogue when they think about screenplays. They are not thinking of structure, the interplay of themes, character arcs, plot points, beats, reversals, pacing, subplots, subtext, the workings of myth and metaphor — in other words, the nuts and bolts that hold stories together. They are thinking of the lines that actors speak. On *Hard Core Logo* the actors were sometimes loose with dialogue, working off of my writing in much the same way that I worked off of Michael Turner's writing. The final product contains maybe seventy to eighty percent of the dialogue that I wrote and not all of this comes out word-for-word as I wrote it. Some wholly improvised moments were created during production and several scripted scenes never made the final cut. The final product is a collaboration among us all — director, cast, book author, film editor, producers, crew, and screenwriter. It's kind of pointless anyway for screenwriters to try and keep score as to "how much" of their work is in a finished film. Films are made under incredible pressure and scripts are subject to all kinds of changes for all kinds of reasons. A decent screenwriter knows that the best screenplay is Zen-like: it bends like a reed as the storm blows, but does not break; if its roots are strong, it will survive without too much damage to its integrity.

A decent screenwriter should also admit that his or her work is often improved by a talented director, cast, and crew. I believe that *HCL* is as good as it is because Bruce McDonald saw well beyond my script to the actual physical reality of the world of a failed rock band, and because our actors discovered a reality that could only be approximated on the script page.

7 January 1997

Take One magazine conducts its Second Annual Film Critics' Poll, a year-end round-up of the best in Canadian cinema. *Hard Core Logo* is chosen as the best Canadian film of 1996, coming ahead of many impressive films that played during the year, including *Crash, Long Day's Journey Into Night, Le confessionnal, Margaret's Museum,* and *Lilies.* Bruce is named best director, in a tie with Robert Lepage. Callum and Hugh come second and third in the best actor category. My script is named best screenplay. The critics' lofty assessment of *HCL* is consistent with the strong reviews the film has had since its appearance at Cannes.

To go by the press, the film has done well and I have done well by it. A few more people return my calls. Funding is a little easier to come by with this new track record. I'm currently plotting another feature film with Bruce. David Griffith and I have a documentary series in the works with the CBC and another feature script in its final stages. I'm making a living at this craft, which is more than I can say for when this diary began. A happy ending? Maybe. But the sorry truth is that *Hard Core Logo* and all these other Canadian films (aside from *Crash*, which has American stars, the whiff of scandal, and some serious promotional muscle behind it) have more or less tanked at the Canadian box office. As *Take One* notes, Canadian films played on less than two percent of available major-chain screens in Toronto in 1996. This is probably better than the national average in English Canada.

We can't even get two percent of our *own* screens in our *own* country?

In most film-producing countries this would be a national scandal. In this country it's greeted with a resigned shrug. Canadians consume so much American pop culture as to be cultural duel citizens. Canadian filmmakers, supported by the government for the time being, aim at originality and generally make marginal, arty, niche-audience films. While we hardly expect to pack suburban sixplexes with this kind of work, it is still frustrating coming to terms with the fact that most Canadian films will barely dent the Canadian cultural consciousness, that they will rarely play anywhere but the big city art-house screens that show foreign films, that here in Canada they practically *are* foreign films.

I wrote in one of this diary's earliest entries that I spend lots of my time plotting my escape to the States. To be honest, I still think about moving. It's a fact of Canadian life that just when people become viable as writers and filmmakers they must weigh the personal cost of remaining in Canada versus the advantages of a career Stateside. The dilemma is dramatized in brutal terms in *Hard Core Logo*: Joe Dick wants to stay put and have a band that does things its own (independent, marginal) way; Billy Tallent does what loads of talented Canadians in music and film have been doing for years and heads south. It occurs to me, in light of the choices faced by many screenwriters and filmmakers, that *Hard Core Logo* (the film, not the book) can be read as an inverted or ironic Atwoodian survival fable. Billy Tallent survives not by being especially resilient, but by turning his back on his home and friends and taking the road south — the road to career viability. Meanwhile, Joe Dick, faced with the failure of his Canadian rock 'n' roll dream in Edmonton, calls it quits and kills himself. At the end of the road, mere survival doesn't cut it any more. Obviously, this is a pessimistic either/or reading of the culture worker's choices in this country, but it effectively illustrates an ongoing dilemma for us. As The Clash put it, "Should I Stay or Should I Go?"

For people like Bruce, who are well enough established, staying in Canada and making films with American or international investors is an option. For the less established, who must try to make films and develop careers with less and less support from government sources, the road south will look more and more attractive in the years ahead. I'm pretty sure I won't take the Joe Dick route and blow my brains out any time soon (I'm sure that Bruce, Hugh, Callum, and Michael Turner won't be putting guns to their heads either). I do know that whatever it takes I'm going to keep writing scripts and making films. Somewhere. Anywhere.

The *Hard Core* crew, 11 November 1995.

THE FOLLOWING PEOPLE AND ANIMALS

would be declared gods if I ran the world. From the *Hard Core Logo* pantheon I thank Bruce McDonald for showing me how to make movies, and for unswerving friendship, support, and generosity through a two-and-a-half-year rollercoaster ride. Without Bruce, this book would not be in your hands. I also thank Michael Turner for starting an interesting chain reaction; Keith Porteous for connecting the right dots; Brian Dennis, Christine Haebler, and Karen Powell for keeping the car on the rollercoaster; John Frizzell for making me think harder; Hugh Dillon, Callum Rennie, Bernie Coulson, John Pyper-Ferguson, and Julian Richings for breathing a hurricane of life into the film; Peter Moore and Swamp Baby for toons that rock supreme; Reg Harkema for editing the real final draft of *Hard Core Logo*; Danny Nowak for making it look so good; Danny Salerno for sharing his ideas about "the making of . . ." (I've only stolen a few); Sandy Kaplansky and Rachel Sutherland at Shadow Shows for all kinds of help; Liane Hentscher for the cool production stills; the rest of the crew and cast of *Hard Core Logo* for five cool weeks in the fall of '95; and Rainbow for a thoroughly convincing performance in a thankless role.

From the *Roadshow* orbit I thank my editor Martha Sharpe for enthusiasm, insight, and skill in helping me beat this beast into shape; my best pal and writing partner David Griffith for key suggestions on how to keep it from sucking; and Anne McDermid for pointing me towards House of Anansi Press.

I also thank my entire family for their unflagging support and curiosity; many good friends for the laughs and loans; and Scout for getting me out twice a day.

Finally, I thank Siobhan O'Flynn and Emma Claire Baker for things so valuable they cannot be put into words.

CREDITS

Photo of Bruce McDonald, p. 6 by Peter Mettler; photo of Michael Turner, p. 11 by Simon Glass (courtesy of Shadow Shows); photo of Noel Baker and Brian Dennis, p. 31 by Bruce McDonald; photo of Julian Richings, p. 34 by Liane Hentscher (all photos by Liane Hentscher courtesy Ed Festus Productions Limited); photo of Callum Rennie, p. 46 by Liane Hentscher; photo of Bernie Coulson, p. 48 by Liane Hentscher; Lick the Pole, p. 49 by Liane Hentscher; Noel, p. 53 by Bruce McDonald; Bruce McDonald and Joey Ramone, p. 68 by Ron Repke; photo of Hugh Dillon, p. 73 by Liane Hentscher; Noel's dog, Scout, p. 109 by Noel Baker; photo of John Pyper-Ferguson, p. 118 by Liane Hentscher; first rehearsal, p. 143 by Noel Baker; "Calgary," p. 153 by Liane Hentscher; the guys, p. 159 by Liane Hentscher; Art Bergmann, p. 162 by Noel Baker; Hard Cores as The Beatles, p. 167 by Liane Hentscher; "Rock 'n' Roll Is Fat and Ugly," p. 169 by Liane Hentscher; Mulligan, p. 174 by Liane Hentscher; Bucky's kitchen, p. 181 by Noel Baker; goat and campfire scene, p. 187 by Liane Hentscher; Hugh with gun, p. 196 by Liane Hentscher; "The Prairies," p. 206 by Noel Baker; Bruce and Danny Nowak, p. 210 by Noel Baker; back of the goat van, p. 218 by Noel Baker; Reg's computer, p. 231 by Liane Hentscher; the crew, page 244 by Liane Hentscher.

Hard Core Logo began as a book by Michael Turner (Vancouver: Arsenal Pulp Press, 1993). *Hard Core Logo* the film was directed by Bruce McDonald (an Ed Festus production, Vancouver/Toronto, 1996). The *Hard Core Logo* Tribute Soundtrack is available on BMG Music Canada, Inc. And there is a comic book *Hard Core Logo* by Nick Craine (Toronto, Black Eye Productions, 1997).